FROM THE SUSQUEHANNA
TO THE TIBER

JEREMY M. CHRISTIANSEN

FROM THE SUSQUEHANNA TO THE TIBER

A Memoir of Conversion from Mormonism to the Roman Catholic Church

IGNATIUS PRESS   SAN FRANCISCO

Cover art:
Spire of the Salt Lake Temple of the Church of Latter-day Saints
Salt Lake City, Utah
©istock/meshphoto

Cover design by Roxanne Mei Lum

© 2022 by Ignatius Press, San Francisco
All rights reserved
ISBN 978-1-62164-592-4 (PB)
ISBN 978-1-64229-255-8 (eBook)
Library of Congress Control Number 2022934528
Printed in the United States of America ∞

*For Our Lady, Saint Thomas More, and
Saint John Henry Newman.
Pray for us.*

The heart is deceitful above all things, and
desperately corrupt; who can understand it?

—*Jeremiah 17:9*

CONTENTS

INTRODUCTION

IT WAS OCTOBER 12, 2015—my wife's birthday, of all days. I still cannot figure out why I told her on her birthday. It was thoughtless. But it had to come out.

Before that moment, I had never said anything to her intimating any doubt about our shared lifelong faith in the Church of Jesus Christ of Latter-day Saints. What had started internally as unease and quiet cognitive dissonance ended with an Earth-shattering revelation: "It isn't true. Whatever else Joseph Smith was, he was not a prophet. Whatever else the Church of Jesus Christ of Latter-day Saints is, it is not what it claims to be."

My wife was stunned and shaken. Her pain was as visceral as mine, but at least mine had come on gradually. Her pain was blindsiding, a sucker punch. Some years later in recollecting that event, she told me one of her first thoughts in that moment: "We can't have any more children, not with this." I had already been saying I was done having children for some time at that point; I was twenty-eight, and we had two boys and two girls. Work, school, ambition, and a mental health episode had overwhelmed me, and I had decided that, as far as I was concerned, our family was complete. For my wife, it was more a matter of sad resignation that our family would now have an irreparable religious rift. In what had to that point been a deeply religious household, more children would only further complicate an increasingly complicated and uncertain life as she worked to preserve and pass on to our children a faith that I resolutely rejected.

My confession broke her heart, but coming to the realization of what I believed—or didn't believe—had broken mine as well. The documentary history of my life in the daily journals I kept between 2005 and 2015 shows only minimal evidence of cracks beginning to form in my faith before it fell apart. The record of the loss of my faith exists mainly in the recesses of my memory; I kept it mostly internal. One day, I record my anticipation of the church's biannual General Conference (in which church leaders speak to the worldwide faith) and express the need to study my "patriarchal blessing", a special transcribed "prophetic" blessing Mormons receive that acts as a sort of blueprint for their life going forward. Less than two weeks later: "It is hard to put it on paper. But I no longer believe in the Church ..."

One thousand one hundred nineteen days after that excruciating evening in our bedroom, my anxious, bewildered, pregnant wife stood toward the back of a small group gathered in the baptistry of Saint Rita Catholic Church in Alexandria, Virginia. Our four children were huddled near her, all of them gawking at the scene: their father, leaning over a font, water poured over his head, then kneeling before a priest and professing belief in the one, holy, Catholic, and Apostolic Church. Immediately after the baptism, I hurried them to a pew near the front where my otherwise very Mormon family witnessed, for the first time, Holy Mass in the extraordinary form of the Roman Rite.

Statuit ei Dóminus testaméntum pacis, et príncipem fecit eum: ut sit illi sacerdótii dígnitas in aetérnum. So chanted the schola as the Introit of the Mass began. The whole scene was alien to the low-church Mormon aesthetic and worship sensibility—altar boys, processional cross, plumes of incense swirling around the large Gothic-style church, women with veils, people bowing toward the priest as he passed up the aisle—all solemn.

As the time for Holy Communion neared, my heart raced, and I kept my hands busy to hide the slight trembling. The priest turned around from the altar and faced everyone, presenting the Host in his hand: *Ecce Agnus Dei. Ecce qui tollit pecáta mundi.* I bowed my head, striking my chest with my fist three times, each time repeating with sincere intensity, *Dómine, non sum dignus, ut intres sub tectum meum: sed tantum dic verbo, et sanábitur ánima mea.* I arose and approached the Communion rail, as the priest had instructed me to go first. I knelt and looked up, my mouth as dry as the Utah deserts to which my pioneer ancestors had come and where I was raised and my Mormon faith was forged, and heard the words *Corpus Dómini nostri Jesu Christi custódiat ánimam tuam in vitam aetérnam. Amen.* I closed my eyes, opened my mouth, and received the Body, Blood, Soul, and Divinity of my Lord.

THE SUSQUEHANNA RIVER stretches more than 450 miles through the northeastern United States, rising in New York and Pennsylvania and emptying into the Chesapeake Bay in Maryland. James Fenimore Cooper, the nineteenth-century Romantic, described it as "one of the proudest rivers of the United States".[1] I was raised to know beyond a shadow of a doubt that on the banks of that river, sometime in 1829, Peter, James, and John—three of Jesus Christ's apostles—had appeared as resurrected and glorified beings to Joseph Smith, the Mormon prophet, and his close associate at the time, Oliver Cowdery, and

---

[1] James Fenimore Cooper, *The Pioneers* (Oxford: Oxford University Press, 1980), 15.

that through the laying on of hands, the apostles had conferred upon them the "keys of the kingdom of heaven" that Peter had received from Christ in Matthew 16:19. This important event restored the priesthood authority that had been lost with the death of the apostles in the first century A.D. and enabled the 1830 organization of the Church of Jesus Christ of Latter-day Saints, the only true and living church on the face of the earth. This church was directed by Jesus Christ himself through continuous revelation to its president, the successor of Joseph Smith, the Mormon prophet, seer, and revelator.

Mine is a journey from the banks of the Susquehanna River to the Tiber of Rome. It is a journey from knowing— beyond a shadow of a doubt—that the Mormon prophet held the keys to God's kingdom on earth to believing that those keys reside with the bishop of Rome, the Vicar of Christ, the Supreme Pontiff—the pope of the Catholic Church. To say that I harbor doubts about the utility for others of reading about my life, which is among the most unexceptional I know of, is to understate my case. Nevertheless, God's Providence is a wondrous thing. He works deeply in the hidden corners of our lives, including those of us who are not significant or famous and who live an ordinary existence, day in and day out. Tracing these workings as I do here may, I pray, help someone in some way. If I am the only beneficiary of this writing, it will still have been worth the time.

This book is also partially a response, and thus somewhat admittedly an *apologia*, to those in my life who have, with all sincerity (and some perhaps without), asked me, "Did you ever really have a testimony of the church?" That term—"testimony"—and its full meaning are critical here. A testimony is a spiritual witness directly from the Holy Ghost, telling you that the Church of Jesus Christ of Latter-day Saints is true and that the church is what it claims to be. This testimony is the foundational building block, the fundamental theological concept, of Mormonism. Indeed, in December 1839, while on a trip to Washington, D.C., to attempt to get the U.S. government to intervene on behalf of the Church of Latter-day Saints, which was facing persecution at the time, President Martin Van Buren is purported to have asked Joseph Smith how the Mormons "differed in [their] religion from the other religions of the day", and Joseph Smith is purported to have answered that Mormons, unlike everyone else, had "the gift of the Holy Ghost".[2]

You can argue until you are blue in the face with a Mormon, but you will make neither heads nor tails of Mormon belief, thought, practice, tradition, or anything else if you fail to understand the importance of "testimony" and the "knowledge" conferred by it within the Mormon paradigm. That experience, or often set of experiences, is so central and so powerful that it holds on to many a Mormon's heart long after his mind has all but left the faith. It feels nearly impossible to reject the Mormon faith once you have a testimony because in doing so, you are rejecting an entire life's worth of transformative experiences that you "know" came from God. Losing that testimony is for many, as the reader may learn from this book, an almost unfathomably disorienting experience that pulls the moral, metaphysical, spiritual, and psychological rug out from under you. Understanding the grip of Mormon testimony is, to my mind, the key to understanding Mormonism *in toto*.

No one can pretend to pure objectivity, and I am no exception. Our attempts to describe our past will always

---

[2] Joseph Smith, *History of the Church of Jesus Christ of Latter-day Saints* (Salt Lake City: Deseret Book, 1978), 4:42.

be colored, at least somewhat, by the lens of the present. That said, I have always been struck by stories of conversion that strive for candor, that put it all out there. You will find no visions, no thunderbolts here. You will only find me laying bare my story as best I can, even when—and maybe particularly when—I find it embarrassing. I have, however, changed the names of certain people from time to time (especially in chapter 2).

One final note on nomenclature. I will use the terms Mormon and Mormon Church as shorthand throughout this book. I am informed that in recent years, the church has begun to take greater exception to the term Mormon. For members of the Church of Jesus Christ of Latter-day Saints who read this, rest assured that I mean no offense by the continued use of a term proudly invoked by me and my ancestors before me for generations. As Joseph Fielding Smith (at the time an apostle and later church president) once observed in defending the use of the name Mormon to leaders of the Reorganized Church of Jesus Christ of Latter-day Saints who had said that "the term Mormon is offensive": "The term 'Mormon' has always been applied to the Church of Jesus Christ of Latter-day Saints", and "during the lifetime of Joseph Smith ... and ever since it has been a term accepted by the Church."[3] Also, officially suggested alternatives, in addition to being cumbersome, tend to be theologically loaded in ways that Mormons ought to understand (for example, the Restored Church), and thus are not likely to be adopted by Christians. But perhaps most important for our purposes here, the use of the term Mormon is immediately recognizable

[3] Joseph Fielding Smith, *Blood Atonement and the Origin of Plural Marriage* (Heber City, UT: Archive Publishers, 1905; repr., Salt Lake City: Deseret News Press, 2000), 11.

to non-Mormon audiences, and my main purpose here is to bridge a gap so that Catholic and Mormon worlds can understand one another.

God bless.

Jeremy Christiansen
Alexandria, Virginia
Feast of the Immaculate Heart of Mary
June 12, 2021

I

Born in the Covenant

"I Nephi, having been born of goodly parents …" So begins the *Book of Mormon*, and so begins the way many Mormons recount their life story. I am no exception, because I was an unexceptional Mormon.

I was born in January 1987 in Monticello, Utah, the sixth of seven children, to two wonderful parents who were and still are devoted to their faith and their family, five boys and two girls in all. We were a modest-sized family in our rural community of Blanding, Utah; there were a fair number of tens and twelves.

My father taught woodshop in the public middle school. My mother stayed at home. Both had college degrees, and my father also had a master's degree. On paper, we were middle-class, I suppose. But perhaps only on paper. During my lifetime, my hometown has increased its population by only 500 people, hovering today around 3,600. The nearest Walmart was over an hour away. When the Taco Bell Express moved into the gas station, well, let me tell you, it was a big deal. In towns like Blanding, you can discern the significance of a community event by whether the codgers at the local NAPA Auto Parts were talking about it—and believe me, they were talking about the Taco Bell Express. It was big.

My father was, unsurprisingly, modestly but sufficiently paid, such that in a rural, out-of-the-way community, if

everything went just right, we'd be fine. But not everything went just right. When I was around ten years old,
my parents faced serious financial struggles. They were
already paying for my oldest brother to serve as a Mormon missionary in Chicago. Extended family and friends
pitched in so that our family could make the regular
payments to keep supporting my brother's mission. But
disaster struck. My younger brother was diagnosed with
ulcerative colitis. Ultimately, he had his entire large intes-
tine removed when he was only eight or nine years old.
He was life-flighted by helicopter the three-hundred-
mile journey to Salt Lake City from our hometown not
once, but twice, for life-threatening postoperative com-
plications. His illness also caused weeks-long stays at Primary Children's Hospital. At times both my parents were
there, while my older siblings and close family friends
cared for us. The stress of that time is not something I
love to reflect on, even after more than twenty years.
We had insurance, but bills associated with this level of
medical care took their toll. My parents had worked hard
to pay off their home mortgage early, but all that was
undone, requiring them to take out a second mortgage
on the house to make ends meet. Then, as a cherry on
top, my oldest sister was diagnosed with multiple sclero-
sis not long after, which required extensive medical testing to diagnose and was yet another emotional blow to
the family. Money was tight, to say the least, and life was
at times overwhelmingly stressful—the idyllic oblivion of
childhood could not keep the family-wide anxiety from
affecting me. Arcadia was elusive.

But my parents managed it all, in no small part due to the
strong Mormon community on which they could lean, both
family and non-family. Mormonism was, and is, everything
to my parents. The sense—and reality—of community in

Mormonism is high, and there is no division between the life of faith and everything else, between Sunday and the rest of the week. It is all integrally woven together.

One of my earliest memories is of my father sick with hepatitis when he was in his thirties and was serving as the bishop of our ward, that is, the lay minister in charge of a Mormon congregation (although this would be a contradiction in terms to Catholics, Mormonism has a "lay priesthood" at the local level). We heated our home with a wood-burning stove. That meant summertime family trips up the mountain to gather firewood to last the winter, followed by predawn wood splitting and fire building to heat the house. When my father fell ill, he was unable even to get out of bed for some time. I recall one gray, cold day being out in the backyard next to the wood pile when a group of men from the ward showed up and spent several hours splitting firewood. My father appeared out the back door in his dark-blue robe, thin and frail, and, a rarity in my memories, visibly emotional.

That was our faith: a life filled with service to others, dedication, and duty to the church. At the center of that life lay the church's traditional teachings and the ever-present goal for which my parents strove, like most other parents in our town and within orthodox Mormon households: that each of their children would gain his own "testimony" that the Mormon Church is God's one true church on earth.

You don't just believe Mormonism. You know it is true. You know that Mormonism is true with a level of epistemological certainty that is hard to describe to an outsider. That is what drives everything; that knowledge is the font of the endless good works of Mormons. The central means of obtaining this knowledge that would then make all other pieces of the faith fall into place was the

Book of Mormon, which was acclaimed by President Ezra Taft Benson, the prophet of the Mormon Church during my earliest years, as the "keystone of our religion".

President Benson made the *Book of Mormon* a center point of his short presidency in the early 1990s. He challenged Mormon families worldwide to read the *Book of Mormon* every day, a practice my faithful parents worked their hardest to implement. When our family finished this challenge, my parents wrote to President Benson to tell him of this accomplishment and the blessings it had brought to our family. President Benson responded with a hand-signed letter congratulating them, a letter that my parents cherished and that my dad hid away in a drawer in his room for safekeeping, a prized family relic.

Near the end of the *Book of Mormon* there is a verse known colloquially as "Moroni's promise". Here, the ancient American prophet Moroni—who would later appear to the Prophet Joseph Smith to reveal to him the location of golden plates containing the ancient record that is the *Book of Mormon*—speaks prophetically to all those who will later read this record. He challenges us: "Now I, Moroni ... would exhort you that when ye shall read these things ... that ye would ask God, the Eternal Father, in the name of Christ, if these things are not true; and if ye shall ask with a sincere heart, with real intent, having faith in Christ, he will manifest the truth of it unto you, by the power of the Holy Ghost. And by the power of the Holy Ghost ye may know the truth of all things."[1] This is the core of Mormonism. This is why it is the way it is, and this is why your Mormon neighbors and friends are the way they are.

Mormons and prospective converts alike are taught that if they are sincere and ask in faith, the Holy Ghost will

[1] *Moroni* 10:1, 4 (from the *Book of Mormon*).

tell them personally that the *Book of Mormon* is true in an identifiable spiritual manifestation. Indeed, any truth can be so confirmed, according to this passage. Thus, upon receiving this spiritual witness, one will know that in fact the *Book of Mormon* is what it purports to be: a historical record of a band of Jews who sailed to the Americas six hundred years before the birth of Christ, knew about Jesus Christ long before his birth through astoundingly specific prophecies, practiced baptism, and were even visited by the resurrected Son of God shortly after he ascended into heaven. These ancient people had living prophets among them, such as Lehi, Nephi, Mosiah, Alma, Mormon, and Moroni. These prophets wrote a spiritual history of their people, which was abridged by the Prophet Mormon and then buried by his son, Moroni, in a hill in upstate New York. On that hill, this same Moroni, sent as a messenger from God centuries later, showed the plates to Joseph Smith in the 1820s, helping usher in the restoration of Christ's true church. That church had been lost from the Earth following the death of Christ's apostles, and Christ's true teachings (those of the Mormon faith) had been quickly corrupted and lost in a Great Apostasy. Joseph Smith, by the gift and power of God, translated these golden plates into the *Book of Mormon*, which was tangible and powerful evidence of Joseph's prophetic calling. This is what is at stake under the framework offered by Moroni.

Mormon leaders have long described the actual experience of the Holy Ghost communicating to you—this confirmation of the truth—as a feeling in which God "will cause that your bosom shall burn within you; therefore, you shall feel that it is right".[2] This is largely (though perhaps not entirely) an emotive experience or, more commonly, a set of emotive experiences over time.

---

[2] *Doctrine and Covenants* 9:8 (Mormon scripture).

Arguably, it amounts to the simultaneous convergence of (1) an abstract truth proposition about the Mormon Church (for example, Joseph Smith was a true prophet, the *Book of Mormon* is the word of God) and (2) an overwhelming emotional sense of wellbeing. Occurring simultaneously, these two things (concept and emotion) produce a powerful "aha!" moment, leading to a sense that one now knows that abstract truth proposition in a distinct and even infallible way. This way of knowing is stronger than knowledge through syllogisms or scientific investigation, because the latter occur through our errant reasoning, while a testimony is a sure witness from God meant as such. That, in essence, is the Mormon testimony. Many Mormons can tell you of some spiritually significant event or series of events when they came to "know" the *Book of Mormon* was true, or when they came to realize they had already known but had not realized it yet. Go ahead and ask them sincerely, and they will be glad to tell you about it in the right setting.

The logic of the matter is presented as follows: if God answers you, through the Holy Ghost, then you know that the *Book of Mormon* is what it purports to be, and everything else falls into place. But while Mormons would describe the *Book of Mormon* as the keystone of their faith, I think that is not quite right. *Testimony* is the keystone. Mormonism rises and falls with the testimonial experience, which serve as the entrée to what Mormonism is really all about: "personal revelation", that is, experiences in which God is personally communicating with you through the Holy Ghost to guide and direct your life according to his unique plan for you.

This testimonial experience is not just a one-time thing. After Mormons are baptized, they receive "Confirmation", in which the "Gift of the Holy Ghost" is given to them (or, perhaps better stated, in which they are told to "receive the Holy Ghost"). This gift is the promise that if you are faithful, the Holy Ghost will constantly guide your life decisions, much as the Holy Ghost provided an answer about the *Book of Mormon*. Every week, when Mormons gather to take the Lord's Supper (what they call "the Sacrament"), the Mormon prayer of consecration states that those who worthily take the Sacrament will "always have [the Lord's] Spirit to be with them". Always. Day and night. Mormon life features this keen emphasis on personal revelation: Mormons confirm important life decisions by seeking some manifestation from the Holy Ghost about what they ought to do, and after they make a decision, they seek confirmation that it is in accordance with God's will. Through this set of experiences, their testimony that "the church is true" is fortified, brick by brick, through the personal revelation of God's guiding hand in their own life and in the life of the church. When church leaders, from the prophet down to the local bishop, make a decision about implementing some program or asking you to undertake some sacrifice, you pray to gain a testimony that the decision is indeed in accordance with God's will—after all, the church's leaders were themselves called to their positions by the process of personal revelation. The central concept of Mormonism is that these experiences will be ever present in your life, continually reaffirming that Mormonism is true.

Our family therefore read the *Book of Mormon* every morning. This was harder to stick to in summertime without the built-in routines of school, but we were remarkably consistent. Our early mornings nearly always included *Book of Mormon* study as a family. We took turns reading a verse each until we finished a chapter or so. That is how I learned to read, cutting my teeth on the *Book of Mormon*'s King James–style English.

Naturally, prayer was also central to our life. After reading a chapter of the *Book of Mormon*, we would kneel as a family for prayers each day. For all of Mormonism's insistence on not having rote prayer, Mormon prayer is almost as predictable as Catholic prayer (almost!) and follows a set pattern: "Dear Heavenly Father, we thank thee for ... We ask thee for ... In the name of Jesus Christ, Amen." The first time it ever occurred to me to pray in earnest for something I really needed was when I was about seven or eight. For about a week, my best friend, Kevin, and I had been secretly playing with matches whenever we could get a chance. One fateful Friday night we took some matches 150 yards across the canal into the fields behind my house to the base of a large tree surrounded by waist-high cheatgrass—as dry as bone. We lit a bundle of grass on fire and tried to stomp it out, but it raced away before we could blink, and in a matter of seconds, flames twenty feet tall roared up the side of that tree, engulfing the tall grass all around it. We bolted back across the canal, and one of us said to the other, "Let's pray." We paused there in the middle of the field to ask God to please get us out of this one—that is, to put out that fire. Firemen ultimately took care of it, and thank God, no one was hurt, nor were any nearby homes damaged. Although I didn't see it this way at the time, I do think God answered our prayer: "*Yes*, I will let you off of this one without real injury to anyone's person or property; *no*, I will not just let you off scot-free." Kevin and I obfuscated for as long as we could about how we had just discovered an enormous fire behind our homes, but it didn't take long for suspicions reasonably to land on us as the unintentional arsonists.

Sundays were for church—which at the time consisted of a three-hour block of meetings. We were never late for church. My father was a punctual person. Mormons don't have assigned seats at church, strictly speaking. But in the Blanding 8th Ward (the congregation whose boundaries covered the southeast portion of our town and its outskirts), you didn't sit in the fifth row from the front on the left-hand side. That is where the Christiansens sat. And the same was more or less true for the dozens of families in our ward, each filing in before the meeting began to take its pew. My memory is of that building being essentially full every week, say, 200 or 250 people, but I'm sure my memory is filling those seats more than they were actually filled at the time. Still, our community was deeply religious.

Church began with Sacrament Meeting. The bishop or one of his counselors—two other laymen called to assist the bishop—would ascend the pulpit, welcome everyone, and announce the opening hymn and who would be giving the opening prayer that day. I grew up saturated in Mormon hymns. My mother always sang, and sang well, and sang loudly. Our home was filled with her singing and the tones of our upright piano. She taught me to sing too. I remember singing "Praise to the Man" when I was seven or eight, a laudatory hymn about Joseph Smith, when my next-door neighbor leaned over and told me what a great voice I had. For whatever reason, I was mortified. My mother made me sing solos now and again, but my nerves always got the better of me, and sometimes those solos got tearful or ended in paralyzing stage fright in front of the entire congregation. She was working hard to help me realize the bit of talent I had and to develop it and overcome fear, for which I am still thankful.

After the opening hymn, there was an opening prayer: "Dear Heavenly Father, we thank thee for ... We ask thee for ... In the name of Jesus Christ, Amen." The bishop or

one of his counselors would make some brief announcements. Perhaps some young man was being ordained to the
next office of the priesthood—boys become "deacons" at
age twelve, "teachers" at fourteen, and "priests" at sixteen.
These are all offices in the "Aaronic priesthood"—the lesser,
preparatory priesthood. They received the "Melchizedek
priesthood" at eighteen and became "elders" or, perhaps, if
called to more serious leadership positions, "high priests".
Or maybe a young woman was advancing to the next program for the young girls, receiving a pendant and some
acknowledgment certificate. "We will now sing hymn
number 193, 'I Stand All Amazed', after which the Aaronic
Priesthood will bless and pass the Sacrament." I thought a
lot about that hymn and what it meant, and I suppose that
is the point of such hymns sung while the Sacrament was
being prepared. It is, of course, not a Mormon hymn, but
it was in the Mormon hymnal at that time.

> Oh, it is wonderful that he should care for me,
> Enough to die for me!
> Oh, it is wonderful, wonderful to me![3]

"Mom," I once asked at a young age, "Why is it wonderful that Jesus *died*? And that they killed him?" I was puz-
zled at how someone's death could be good in some sense
for me, and why we would celebrate it.

During the Sacrament hymn, whatever it might be on
a given Sunday, I often looked up behind the pulpit and
the choir seats to a large painting that hung at the head of
the chapel—which would be an oddity for Mormon chapels today, but our church was built around 1905 and was

[3] Charles Hutchinson Gabriel, "I Stand All Amazed", in *Hymns* (Salt Lake
City: Church of Jesus Christ of Latter-day Saints, 1985), 193, https://www
.churchofjesuschrist.org/music/library/hymns/i-stand-all-amazed?lang=eng.

architecturally interesting. The painting was hung sometime in the 1950s, before "correlation" in the church (a
time when a powerful church committee in Salt Lake City
began standardizing everything from Sunday school lessons
to acceptable colors of carpet). Artwork is no longer hung
in Mormon chapels, being limited to hallways and lobbies,
but the church had sort of grandfathered in artwork that
had long been in place and whose removal would likely
cause serious upheaval in local congregations. So it was
with our chapel and the massive painting entitled *Jesus and
Children*. Today it is part of Standard Publishing's Classic
Bible Art Collection. That image is indelibly inscribed in
my consciousness, and I studied it countless times as my
mind wandered during countless Sunday services.

White-shirted twelve- and thirteen-year-old boys wearing ties, the deacons all sit together at the front left of the
room. They stand up in unison and file up to the Sacrament table, where three sixteen-year-olds (the priests) stand,
having already torn up off-brand Wonder Bread during the
Sacrament hymn and placed the small pieces on stainless
steel trays. The priest in the middle kneels down, slides out a
built-in microphone that hums over the speakers, and prays,
"O God, the Eternal Father, we ask thee in the name of thy
Son, Jesus Christ, to bless and sanctify this bread to the souls
of all those who partake of it, that they may eat in remem-
brance of the body of thy Son, and witness unto thee, O
God, the Eternal Father, that they are willing to take upon
them the name of thy son, and always remember him, and
keep his commandments which he has given them, that
they may have his Spirit to be with them. Amen."[4]

---

[4] "Blessing on the Bread", The Church of Jesus Christ of Latter-day Saints,
accessed March 18, 2022, https://abn.churchofjesuschrist.org/study/scriptures
/sacrament/bread?lang=eng.

"Amen", says the whole congregation in unison. The priest looks over to the bishop, who shakes his head and twiddles his fingers in a "do it again" motion. You see, it was the "may have" at the end. That was wrong. The proper words are "that they may *always* have his Spirit to be with them". Babies are crying, but their parents take them to the soundproof cry rooms that flank the chapel on either side. "O God", the priest begins again. This time he gets it right. One deacon takes his tray from the priest and walks to the bishop, who takes a piece of bread and eats it. Then the priests take bread from the trays the deacons are holding and eat. The deacons then fan out and give bread to everyone in the congregation who is disposed to eat it—a symbol by which members of the church renew their covenants with God.

Once, one of my older brothers did not take the bread when the tray was passed down the pew to him; he passed the tray on to me. It was palpably uncomfortable for me. After church my dad came to my room, knocked on the door, and asked, with visible distress, "Did [your brother] take the Sacrament?" It was rare to see people not taking the Sacrament, and for a parent to see his child not taking it would be a definite red flag.

The deacons return their trays to the priests and take a piece of bread themselves, and the priests cover the bread trays by folding a large white linen over them. Then the priests fold up the opposite side of the sheets, exposing stainless steel trays with individual little cup holders, probably two or three dozen per tray, each with a tiny clear plastic cup like an oversized thimble filled with water. Two priests shuffle positions, and the priest now in the middle kneels down, saying, "O God", and pronounces a similar prayer over the water. I saw that ritual essentially every week for almost thirty years.

After the Sacrament, the bishop or whichever of his counselors was conducting the service that Sunday would announce the speakers, who, when I was young, were frequently entire families. The smallest children might just recite a verse of Scripture that an adult or an older sibling whispered in their ear. Older children had short prepared speeches on some chosen topic. Families that were musically inclined would often break up the numerous discourses with a special musical number.

Once a month, generally the first Sunday, was a "fast and testimony" meeting. Instead of talks assigned by the bishop, it was a sort of open mic event in which members of the ward got up to bear their testimonies of the truthfulness of the Mormon Church. The first portion was always reserved for children. One by one, they would line up at the front and nervously approach the microphone. "I'd like to bear my testimony, I know the church is true, I know Ezra Taft Benson is a true prophet, I know Joseph Smith was a prophet, I know the *Book of Mormon* is true, I know that families can be together forever, in the name of Jesus Christ, Amen"—one breathless statement after another. Then the adults would go. Many times the speeches devolved into travel logs, emotional expressions of love for their families, and repeated statements of the phrase "I know, with every fiber of my being, that the church is true" or similar assertions of each person's unsurpassed certainty.

After each meeting, which ended with another hymn and a closing prayer by another member of the congregation, we would all shuffle off either to primary school, for those under age twelve, or to Sunday school, for those twelve and above (with classes divided up by general age ranges). In the third hour were gender-segregated meetings for further lessons. In these weekly meetings, local congregation members assigned to teach reinforced the foundational Mormon teachings I learned at home from my parents. There was a consistent, central founding narrative on which our testimonies rested: a canonized retelling of the founding of the church, penned in 1838 by Joseph Smith and his close associates.

According to this account, in the spring of 1820, Joseph Smith, just fourteen years old, was confused over the many religions he saw around him in his rural upstate New York community. There was at the time a great religious revival. He heard various ministers of the Methodist, Baptist, and Presbyterian Churches contend with one another for converts, preaching contradictory interpretations of the Bible, each claiming the truth for itself. Joseph's own family was caught up in the revival, with his family members joining different churches. What was Joseph to do?

One day, while reading his Bible, Joseph came across James 1:5: "If any man lack wisdom, let him ask of God, that giveth to all men liberally, and upbraideth not; and it shall be given him" (KJV). The passage of Scripture struck Joseph Smith to his core, more so than any passage of Scripture he had ever read. He ultimately decided to go into the woods and pray vocally to ask God which of all the churches was the true one that he should join, because it had never occurred to him that they might all be wrong.

On a clear morning, early in the spring of 1820, Joseph knelt in a grove of trees near his home and began to pray when he was suddenly seized by a wicked unseen force that bound his tongue and would not permit him to speak. He was wrestling with the demonic force, feeling as though he might die, when, in desperation, he cried out to God in his heart. In the canonized 1838 account of his "First Vision", he described what happened next:

I saw a pillar of light exactly over my head, above the brightness of the sun, which descended gradually until it fell upon me. It no sooner appeared than I found myself delivered from the enemy which held me bound. When the light rested upon me I saw two Personages, whose brightness and glory defy all description, standing above me in the air. One of them spake unto me, calling me by name and said, pointing to the other—"This is My Beloved Son. Hear Him!" My object in going to inquire of the Lord was to know which of all the sects was right, that I might know which to join. No sooner, therefore, did I get possession of myself, so as to be able to speak, than I asked the Personages who stood above me in the light, which of all the sects was right (for at this time it had never entered into my heart that all were wrong)— and which I should join. I was answered that I must join none of them, for they were all wrong; and the Personage who addressed me said that all their creeds were an abomination in his sight; that those professors were all corrupt; that: "they draw near to me with their lips, but their hearts are far from me, they teach for doctrines the commandments of men, having a form of godliness, but they deny the power thereof." He again forbade me to join with any of them.[5]

Thus, with a glorious theophany, the restoration of the fullness of the Gospel of Jesus Christ had begun! And in this astounding first vision, key truths lost to so-called Christianity began to be re-revealed, including that God the Father and Jesus Christ were distinct, separate, *physical*

[5] "Joseph Smith's First Vision", The Church of Jesus Christ of Latter-day Saints, accessed March 18, 2022, https://www.churchofjesuschrist.org/manual /the-testimony-of-the-prophet-joseph-smith/joseph-smiths-first-vision?lang =eng#:~:text=It%20no%20sooner%20appeared%20than,above%20me%20in%20 the%20air.

beings, a concept that brought revolutionary clarity to the idea that man was made in God's image.

Things quieted down after that for a few years, but God had a plan for Joseph. In September 1823, while he was in deep prayer and reflection one night in his bedroom, an angel appeared to Joseph Smith. He said his name was Moroni, that God was calling Joseph Smith to a special work, and that in a hill near Joseph's home was buried an ancient record of Scripture, engraved on golden plates. These golden plates contained the fullness of Christ's Gospel, and Joseph was called to translate them as part of his prophetic mission to restore Christ's true teachings to the Earth.

For several years, Joseph would visit the hill on the same day and converse with the angel Moroni, who would instruct and prepare Joseph for this important calling. Joseph was permitted to look inside a stone box buried in the hill, and there they were—golden plates, along with what looked like an ancient pair of glasses, two crystal stones set in metal rims called the Urim and Thummim (see Exodus 28:30), which were to be used to translate the sacred work.

In September 1827, Joseph was finally spiritually prepared to fulfill his mission. He retrieved the golden plates from the hill and set about translating them by the gift and power of God. I can't count the times my primary teachers, or some church publication, depicted Joseph, sitting quietly with his scribe, looking over the golden plates with his brow furrowed, as God showed him word by word what was written on the plates and Joseph then dictated those words to his scribe. More miraculous still, despite the fact that Joseph Smith had essentially no formal education, in a period of only a couple of months, he produced what could only be described as a marvelous work and a wonder, proof of his prophetic calling—the *Book of Mormon.*

This scriptural record documented the travels of ancient peoples from the Middle East to the American continent, including their spiritual and temporal rises and downfalls. These people were, as the *Book of Mormon*'s introduction said and as the church taught, "the principal ancestors of the American Indians".[6] These ancient Jews fled Jerusalem before the Babylonian captivity around 600 B.C. The patriarch of this family was named Lehi. He traveled across the ocean, along with his wife, his daughters, his sons Laman, Lemuel, Nephi, and Sam, and another family, and built a great civilization here, somewhere in the Americas. Laman and Lemuel were wicked and obstinate, unlike their younger brother Nephi, who was faithful. After the death of their father Lehi, the group cleaved in two, with the Lamanites following Laman, and the Nephites following Nephi, the former group generally wicked and the latter group generally righteous. Indeed, to set them apart from one another, God cursed the Lamanites with dark skin.

God sent prophets among these two groups over the course of centuries, and the groups struggled to keep God's commandments, engaged in wars, and so on. In the pinnacle event of the *Book of Mormon*, the resurrected Jesus Christ appears to the Nephite people shortly after he ascended into heaven in the Holy Land, teaching them personally. Although these people lived righteously for hundreds of years after that event, they ultimately became wicked, with the Lamanites killing off the Nephites in a series of battles in which millions of people died. The lone

[6] Introduction to *The Book of Mormon* (Salt Lake City: Church of Jesus Christ of Latter-day Saints, 1981).

survivor of the Nephite race was Moroni, who took the plates (which were in part handed down from ancestors) and buried them in a hill in modern-day New York, where Joseph Smith would later find them at Moroni's direction when he appeared as an angel in the 1820s.

Not only was the *Book of Mormon* God's word, like the Bible, and a powerful testimony of Jesus Christ, but it also restored many truths that were part of Christ's original teachings, but that had been lost, or worse, intentionally removed from the Bible by "the Church of the Devil", as the *Book of Mormon* itself explains (and, while it was not polite to say anymore, we all kind of knew that church leaders had once taught explicitly that this "Church of the Devil" was the Roman Catholic Church). The *Book of Mormon* was "the most correct book" of all books on the face of the earth, and reading it daily was critical to our salvation and to ensuring that we had a testimony.

With the *Book of Mormon* published in 1830, Joseph Smith began making converts who read the *Book of Mormon* and became convinced through the Holy Ghost that it was true. God began giving more and more revelations to Joseph to restore fully God's kingdom to what it had been in the past; these revelations were compiled in the *Book of Commandments*, which was later renamed *Doctrine and Covenants*. As a part of this marvelous restoration, God sent John the Baptist as a heavenly messenger to ordain Joseph Smith and his associate Oliver Cowdery with the Aaronic priesthood, a form of authority to work in God's name that had been lost from the earth during the Great Apostasy. Then, sometime later, Peter, James, and John appeared to Joseph Smith and Oliver Cowdery on the banks of the Susquehanna River and conferred on them the Melchizedek priesthood, the higher priesthood, which would permit them to act in God's name to administer saving ordinances for mankind and to restore and organize God's one true church on Earth. On April 6, 1830, that church was organized and is now known as the Church of Jesus Christ of Latter-day Saints.

We believed that Joseph was, as all true prophets, maligned and persecuted by wicked people bent on his destruction. He suffered for the truth over and again. For example, on one harrowing night, Joseph was dragged from his bed in the dead of night by an angry mob that tried to poison him—chipping his tooth on a glass vial of poison they tried to force into his mouth—and then tarred and feathered him because of his religion. The draft from the cold got to the twin children he and his devoted wife Emma had just adopted, eventually killing them both. As Joseph Smith would say himself, he was "called to swim in deep waters".

But the truth of the Restoration simply couldn't be held back. It was God's work. The Saints (that is, the early church members) moved to Kirtland, Ohio. God then told Joseph Smith to build a temple, in which sacred ordinances would be revealed for man's salvation. These ordinances were initially revealed there, but only in part. In 1836, in Kirtland, Ohio, Elijah the prophet appeared to Joseph Smith in the temple and restored to him the "sealing power" of the priesthood.

Immense persecutions continued, ultimately forcing the Saints to Nauvoo, Illinois. There, Joseph received the fullness of the temple rituals, known as the Temple Endowment, and the Sealing Ordinance whereby families could be sealed together forever through the New and Everlasting Covenant of Marriage. He had also translated ancient Egyptian papyri by this time, which resulted in the publication of the *Book of Abraham*, an account written by Abraham himself that revealed the details of God's "Plan of Salvation".

With the temple and these other materials, Joseph restored to the Earth the knowledge that we are "spirit" children of God, our Heavenly Father, and—although she was too sacred to talk about—a Heavenly Mother as well. We had lived as spirits with them before the world was created. God presented us a beautiful plan in which we would come to Earth to be tested and to obtain physical bodies, just like he had. This life was a test, and if we were true and faithful to the covenants we made with God throughout life, at baptism and in the temple, we would return to heaven with our families, all "sealed" together. In heaven, husband and wives would become just like our Heavenly Father and Mother—we would become *gods*, and the pattern would continue forever. This was not just "salvation"; it was "exaltation". One of our Heavenly Father's children, Lucifer, volunteered to be our savior—for God knew we would commit sins and make mistakes during our time on Earth that would impede us from returning to him—but Lucifer's suggestion came at the cost of our freedom of choice. Under his plan, we would be forced to be righteous, and he therefore promised that none of God's children would be lost. Lucifer further stipulated that all the glory of this outcome should be his. But God's oldest spirit child, Jehovah (Jesus Christ), volunteered to be our savior and suffer for our sin to permit all of us freely to choose whether to obey God's commandments or not, and declared that all glory would go to God. God chose Jehovah's plan, which angered Lucifer, and one-third of God's spirit children sided with Lucifer and were all cast out of heaven. Lucifer became Satan, who, along with the other cast-out spirit children of God, seeks to tempt us to sin and keep us from getting back to our heavenly parents.

Joseph Smith's enemies continued their unjust persecution. Ultimately, he was falsely imprisoned in Carthage,

Illinois, and an angry anti-Mormon mob killed him on June 27, 1844. He was a martyr, but God's work rolled on. Countless times I heard the following passage, which is canonized Scripture for Mormons and which was penned as a eulogy for Joseph Smith shortly after his death: "Joseph Smith, the Prophet and Seer of the Lord, has done more, save Jesus only, for the salvation of men in this world than any other man that ever lived in it."[7] That was who Joseph Smith was to me.

Following Joseph's martyrdom, the Saints followed Brigham Young across the plains to Salt Lake City— except, for some reason, Emma Smith, Joseph's wife. She couldn't find it in her to leave her home, so she stayed in the Midwest and never came to Utah. But once the Saints were gathered in Utah, God established Zion, and one after another, God called new prophets to lead the one true church on the face of the Earth, up to my time with Ezra Taft Benson, then Gordon B. Hinckley, and so on.

The prophet spoke to God. The teachings of the modern, living prophet were more important than all the Scriptures combined, because the prophet received continuing revelation from God on how to lead the church today. There were many stories of modern prophets seeing Jesus Christ face to face. Lorenzo Snow, for example, saw Jesus Christ in the Salt Lake City temple and conversed with him. Sacred experiences like this were not to be shared lightly, or usually at all. Twice a year we would sit for hours at a time to listen to the prophet and the apostles of the church in the church's General Conference, and over and over, we would hear of the "special witness" of these men; they were "special witnesses" of Jesus Christ. We all knew what that meant. To be an

[7] *Doctrine and Covenants* 135:3.

apostle in the New Testament (or so I was taught) was to have *seen* Jesus, and *that* is what made the testimony of these men "special". As a child in primary, I sang with all the other kids innumerable times:

> Follow the prophet, follow the prophet,
> Follow the prophet; don't go astray.
> Follow the prophet, follow the prophet,
> Follow the prophet; he knows the way.[8]

Only by doing that could I be assured of salvation and exaltation in the Celestial Kingdom of God, the highest degree of heaven that only those who have received all of the Mormon Church's ordinances and have faithfully kept the covenants associated with those ordinances could enter.

The first of these ordinances was, of course, baptism. Mormons do not baptize until age eight. Passages in the *Book of Mormon* condemn infant baptism as "gross error" (*Moroni* 8:6), "solemn mockery before God" (8:9), "awful wickedness" (8:19), and "perver[sion]" (8:16), adding that anyone who "supposeth that little children need baptism is in the gall of bitterness and in the bonds of iniquity", has "neither faith, hope, nor charity" (8:14), "denieth the mercies of Christ, and setteth at naught the atonement" (8:20), and that all such who would even entertain the thought "are in danger of death, hell, and an endless torment" (8:21). So when I was eight, I was old enough to choose to be baptized. My oldest brother, Jon, baptized me (I wanted him to, and I've always been close to him). The next day I received Confirmation, during which priesthood holders put their hands on my head and conferred on me "the Gift

---

[8] Duane E. Hiatt, "Follow the Prophet", in *Children's Songbook*, ed. The Church of Jesus Christ of Latter-day Saints (Salt Lake City: Church of Jesus Christ of Latter-day Saints, 1989), 110.

of the Holy Ghost". *Now* I had the possibility of *always* having the Holy Ghost with me to testify to me about what was true and what was not, and to lead me throughout my life. My mother spoke at my baptism and told me how important what would happen the next day was, when I would receive the Gift of the Holy Ghost. She had in her arms a blanket my grandmother had made for me when I was young and which I still slept with at the time. It was white, with brown teddy bears, red hearts, and red trim. During her talk, she told me to come up in front of everyone, and as she explained the gift of the Holy Ghost, she told me it would be like this, wrapping the blanket around me tightly, making me feel warm and safe inside. That is how I could know when the Holy Ghost was speaking to me.

Monday nights were for "family home evening", a family devotional time. Someone conducted it, sounding just like a bishop in Sacrament meeting. We had opening and closing prayers, opening and closing songs, a Scripture recitation, a lesson, a game, and a treat. Wednesday nights were for "mutual", youth activities such as Boy Scouts and the church's programs for young women. We had ward parties every so often throughout the year where the Jell-O salad flowed freely.

Every adult had a "calling", an assignment, received by revelation from God through the bishop, as to what cog (and I say that not in a disparaging way) in God's great mechanism one was to be at the time. My parents served faithfully, devoting hours upon hours of their free time to being faithful, active Mormons who did their best, and, despite it all, always—and I mean always—paid 10 percent of their income as tithing to the church. My parents *never* failed to pay their tithing, no matter how difficult times were. Indeed, the worse things seemed financially, the surer they were that they must pay their tithing, and God would, as his prophets of old and in the modern day have promised repeatedly, "open the windows of heaven" (3 Nephi 24:10), pouring forth blessings so great there would not be room to receive them all.

Every so often, my parents would leave on a long weekend trip to go to the temple in Manti, Utah. That was the nearest temple to us. To this day I cannot figure out why it never occurred to me to ask or think what it was my parents, and the other parents from the neighborhood and ward who would go, were doing there. Even as a child in primary, singing the song "I love to see the Temple. I'll go inside someday",[9] it just never really occurred to me to think, "What is this all about?" I only knew it was "sacred", which meant it was not to be spoken of, and that it involved making covenants with God. Yet at the same time, all the time I was growing up, there was some underlying sense of some knowledge just beyond the horizon. I became more bookish as I got older, and I read an important Mormon theological book called *Jesus the Christ*, which said that God's personal name was Elohim. I asked my mother about where that comes from or how we know that (because it does not appear in Mormon Scripture), and she affirmed that it was true and that it was something learned in the temple.

The overwhelming majority of those who lived in our little community were Mormon. Accordingly, as a young boy, I only had two brief encounters with Christianity, neither of which is pleasant to recall.

The first was with my friend Paul when I was probably five or six. His family were some sort of "Christians", he would tell me. I wasn't really sure what that was or

---

[9] *Children's Songbook*, 95.

what that meant. Paul once gave me a small unadorned brass cross, probably three inches or so in length. It seemed important to him, and I vaguely remember him providing some sense to me that it was connected with being a Christian. But to me its real worth lay in my imagination, which fashioned it as the Cross of Coronado, the bedazzled crucifix from *Indiana Jones and the Last Crusade*, my favorite movie as a kid. When I showed my parents, making sure to emphasize how cool it was that I could now more authentically recreate the scenes from the movie in my playtime alongside my makeshift Holy Grail, they were aghast. "We don't use crosses or have them in our homes. That is the weapon used to kill Jesus. If our best friend had been stabbed with a knife or shot with a gun, surely we wouldn't hang up a knife or gun to remember the event or wear a necklace of one, either, so we don't use crosses." They told me I had to give it back. I remember feeling like I had done something very wrong.

The second interaction with Christianity in my youth is one that haunts me to this day and that I recount shamefully, but in the spirit of honesty. I was in first grade at the time. A young boy named Samuel moved in down the street. He was a Baptist. My best friend and I chased him for it, threatening to beat him up. He yelled, in a rather thick Southern accent, that he was going to tell his pastor. "What is a pastor?" I thought to myself as I mounted the kid to sock him in the face for no other reason than being Baptist, whatever that meant. He was down on a large dirt mound in the field across from my best friend's house. Just as I was about to deck him, a gigantic hand grabbed me by the neck and lifted me off the ground. It was my Mormon neighbor, Big John Hughes. All the Hugheses were big, with hearts (and tempers) to match. John chided me for discriminating against Samuel in such an ugly way. I guess he could hear what we were yelling. Samuel moved away by the next year. I never saw him again. I am sure it was difficult for his parents to move in and have their son, a religious minority, tormented by the local Mormon kids—who belonged to the one true church, mind you— simply by virtue of the *name* Baptist, not for anything he had done. This story is one I have forced into the furthest recesses of my mind. I am overcome with shame writing it down. My parents did not raise me that way and would have been horrified by what I did.

Those were the earliest interactions with Christians that I can recall. These interactions reinforced the sense of Mormon distinctiveness I was raised with. If I was taught and learned nothing else growing up, it was that we, as members of the Church of Jesus Christ of Latter-day Saints, were different from everyone else in the world. We had the answers. We had the Restored Gospel.

2

Hold to the Rod

IN ONE OF THE EARLY CHAPTERS of the *Book of Mormon*, the ancient Israelite prophet Lehi has a vision of a tree of life, representing God's love and offering of eternal life. Leading up to this tree is a straight and narrow path, with an iron rod running alongside it. An angel later explains to Lehi's son Nephi, who is permitted to see this vision as well, that this iron rod represents the word of God. In the vision, all those who hold to the rod make it to the tree; those who do not are lost in a mist of darkness, or worse, fall into a deep ravine pining after a "great and spacious building" on the other side of the ravine, which is full of people mocking and pointing their fingers at those who are holding to the iron rod. A popular Mormon hymn based on this *Book of Mormon* vision sermonizes:

> Hold to the rod, the iron rod;
> 'Tis strong, and bright, and true.
> The iron rod is the word of God;
> 'Twill safely guide us through.[1]

As a teenager, I began to let go.

---

[1] "The Iron Rod", in *Hymns*, ed. The Church of Jesus Christ of Latter-day Saints (Salt Lake City: Church of Jesus Christ of Latter-day Saints, 1985), 274.

In those years, I lived a double life. On the one hand, I basically always attended church and religious instruction during the release time in high school (which for Mormons is called seminary) and participated in the youth activities during the week, especially Boy Scouts. I earned my Eagle Scout award. I was a camp counselor at a Boy Scout leadership training camp for four summers in a row. I got to be a good kid at those camps, and they definitely had a good influence on me. The adult leaders, the other young men who were on the staff, were good people, and part of me recognized the goodness of their lives. They taught the virtues of family, faith, home, patriotism, hard work, responsibility, and clean living.

But from age thirteen to eighteen, I walked precariously, with one foot in a countercultural lifestyle that grew increasingly dangerous and risky and one foot in the Mormon Church. The only way I managed to keep my worlds from colliding was by lying. I didn't really care. I did what I thought I had to to keep my life the way I wanted it.

As is common at the age of thirteen or fourteen, my life started to change as I spent more and more time with friends outside my home and neighborhood. Something men of the millennial generation almost all remember is when—not whether, but when—they first saw pornography. My encounters with it were typical for my generation, which came of age straddling two different worlds: the one before the internet and the one after. I was in seventh grade when I first watched porn. I was at the house of an older friend, Isaac, and his parents were gone. Isaac told me and my best friend at that time, Charles, that he had a VHS cassette that his dad had hidden away somewhere and that he had found. A mix of curiosity, peer pressure, lack of courage, rebellion, and a strong dose of hormones converged, and Charles and I both said, "Sure." Within a few minutes, I was watching hardcore porn and still remember thinking to myself, "So this is it, huh?"

A range of feelings swept through me at the time, including a deep sense of guilt, though not enough to stop me from doing it or to get me to amend my ways. Alongside the impression that what I was watching was wrong was the notion that I was growing up, rejecting what I had learned at home, becoming my own person—in addition to the obvious feelings that go along with porn use. The realization that such things could be found now simply by searching on the internet rather than getting old videotapes recorded from the forbidden channels of the satellite dish by someone's older brother necessarily led to increased use. Without dwelling too much on this point, I think it is worth mentioning that a memoir of just about any Christian male's life in the West in the twenty-first century that skips over the reality of pornography is quite possibly telling a carefully curated falsehood. Of all the boys I knew growing up, whose families ran the gamut from hyperactive Mormons to not Mormon at all and everything in between, I only knew *one* who had not looked at it at least once. A sense that pornography was wrong always nagged at me, but I let habit and selfishness overcome my judgment.

At that early point, however, I also soothed my conscience with the thought that whatever wrongs I was dallying with, I had not crossed over into the *really* bad stuff: violating the "Word of Wisdom". This was the name of a revelation that Joseph Smith claimed to have received in the 1830s. On its face, the revelation does not actually prohibit anyone from doing anything, but rather is couched in terms of a strong suggestion from God with accompanying blessings for keeping it. What is more, on its face, the revelation only suggests that liquor, tobacco, and "hot drinks" (understood at the time as tea and coffee) were not to be ingested—it expressly permits beer and at least sacramental wine. Within Mormonism, the Word of Wisdom was hardly mandatory until around the early twentieth century. At that time, it was also interpreted as prohibiting the use of all alcohol, tobacco, coffee, and tea, and leaders later added illegal drugs to the list. The Word of Wisdom became a strong marker of Mormon identity, setting Mormons apart much like Jewish kosher observance or Catholic abstinence from meat on Fridays. Although it is not official church teaching, many people I know who were raised in the Mormon stronghold communities in Utah agree that the Word of Wisdom served as a sort of proxy for a person's moral character. Sexual sin was bad, but even some of the good kids fell prey to lust from time to time. Sexual sin was no small matter, but in my town and in countless towns like it, the *bad* kids and *bad* people, with whom one should not associate, were the ones who smoke or drank. I am not suggesting that this is what the church actually teaches, but it is in practice the way many people instinctively feel and act in rural Mormon communities.

I resisted opportunities to drink alcohol with older friends for some time, but I suppose that running in the crowd I was in, it was only a matter of time before I changed my thinking. At some point during my freshman year of high school, I had committed in my own mind to getting drunk. At first, I opted for a home experiment— trying to make some wine for myself with grape juice and yeast. Let's just say that one didn't work out. I would need more than my own lights to pull this one off. So one weekend, I found out that my older friend TJ—who lived in my ward boundaries just around the corner from my house, and with whom I occasionally played hooky to skip Sunday school—had the house to himself. His parents were gone. We were hanging out at his house with James and Adam, also older buddies, on a Saturday afternoon watching *Full Metal Jacket*. I knew James and Adam were planning on drinking that night, and I pulled out a $20 bill and gave it to James, who assured me that they had someone who could get us some beer (I believe it was a twenty-something named Rick, with whom I would later fall in more and more). There was a church dance that Saturday night, the perfect excuse to be out late with friends, and we could hang out at TJ's house.

James and Adam picked me up around six or seven P.M., and we drove in James' white pickup truck to a secluded spot north of town, near a large reservoir: a spot where kids could party with a reasonable hope that no one would come off-roading to find them, including and especially the police. We left the paved road and went down a dirt trail in the truck until we dropped into a small ditch surrounded with juniper trees. We hopped out, and James pulled out a twelve pack of Coors Light from behind the seat of his truck. He handed one to me. I cracked it open and took a long swig. I was unimpressed with the taste but lied about that, as I imagine most teenagers do when they first drink beer. I was fourteen years old and probably 150 pounds, so it didn't take many cans, even with Utah's beer at the time, which was limited to 3.2 percent alcohol, before I was pretty well drunk and earned my high school nickname, Stumbly. We drove back into town and over to TJ's house for a while. Then we headed to the church dance, which was outside in the parking lot because of the good weather. A friend of mine, Stacy, who wasn't a partier but who was part of our circle and didn't care, said within about five seconds of me saying hi, "Jeremy, you're drunk."

My friend Kasey was the first of our group of friends to start drinking with the older guys like James and Adam. Then I started. We both got our friend Charles to join in one night. We all drove to the gravel pits outside of town, where we unloaded a large case of Zima and everyone started drinking. At one point, we heard a truck coming along the top ridge of the gravel pit, and we could see it had a spotlight and was looking down—we all assumed it was the cops, and everyone scattered, hiding behind ten-foot-tall piles of gravel or whatever else they could find. Turns out it was a group of some of the "good" kids out spotlighting the night before opening day of the deer hunting season. They had a rifle on them (which is illegal—you can't spotlight with a firearm in your possession), and they seemed like they might have been trying to poach the night before the legal season began. They were spooked because they thought *we* were game wardens out sitting around looking for poachers on the eve of rifle season. Because we caught one another in equally compromising situations, a tacit, bilateral nondisclosure agreement was immediately in place, *de facto*.

To this day I deeply regret having goaded Charles into coming with us that night. Unlike Kasey and I, who were able to pull our lives together much earlier, Charles' life took bad turn after bad turn, landing him in serious drug addiction and prison for a while. I hear he is doing well now, but he had some harsh years. And I always took some responsibility for that. I told him that once through the glass at the San Juan County jail. But he insisted to me that he owned his conduct. He was obviously right in some sense, and so was I in another.

For us, drinking required a significant amount of effort. To begin with, we lived in a dry town—alcohol was not sold anywhere in city limits. You could only buy beer at the small gas station called Shirt Tail, about five miles south of town. To get liquor or wine, you had to go twenty minutes north to Monticello, where the nearest state-owned liquor store was. And, of course, as a teen-ager, I had to rely on shadowy adult figures like Rick who were willing to buy alcohol for us.

I resisted marijuana for a while and was even vocal about it, but curiosity got the better of me on July 24, 2002. It was Pioneer Day, a Utah state holiday that is as big as the Fourth of July, celebrating the day the Mormon pioneers entered the Salt Lake valley in 1847. After spending the day at the county fair with my friend Ethan, we drove to his house—his parents were gone—and we crouched in the stairwell to the basement entrance as he loaded the weed into a homemade pipe fashioned from a Diet Coke can. Then we watched *Falling Down* in his family's home theatre.

Even before that, though, I had decided on my drug of choice: opiate painkillers. I didn't realize it then, but I was part of the mass crowd of rural Americans with far too easy access to highly addictive painkillers. I took them any chance I got and secured them by hook or crook (I'll plead the Fifth on the details).

I always fancied myself the most reasonable of our tight circle of delinquents, and I often acted as a sort of mother hen, attempting to prevail as the voice of reason in this or that scenario. It just never made sense to me why people would smoke weed and then go to public places where it was obvious to everyone that they were high. I would remind my friends that maybe, just maybe, waltzing into the high school basketball game on a Friday night completely drunk when a fourth of the town is present, including numerous police officers, was not such a hot idea. This is not to say I didn't engage in risky behavior or that I had not begun to form an identity within the drug culture. To the contrary, to some degree it swallowed my life up just like it did my friends' lives. We spent our time watching drug movies like *Dazed and Confused*, *Half Baked*, *Fear and Loathing in Las Vegas*, *Requiem for a Dream*, *Spun*, *Blow*, and the like. It fueled reckless behavior for all of us, me included.

Through some internet research, I discovered that opiates are water soluble, while acetaminophen (the part of painkillers that is just ordinary Tylenol and doesn't get you high) is not. Thus, I worked out that I could crush up painkillers, dissolve them in water as much as they would come apart, filter the acetaminophen out with a coffee filter, and evaporate the remaining water with a candle warmer. The leftover crystals were potent stuff that we would chop up into fine powder and snort. Lortab, Vicodin, Percocet, and the granddaddy of them all, Oxycontin—I couldn't number how many of those pills I swallowed or snorted. My friend Burt stole vials of morphine from his mother. I never had the guts to shoot it up, so I broke off the top of the vials and drank every obscenely bitter drop. The lack of supply was really the only thing that stopped me from becoming highly addicted. But I had my fair share of withdrawal pains after a long binge.

Another time I took an enormous amount of a prescription muscle relaxer called Soma while I was at school. Within a short amount of time, I realized I had made a mistake. An overpowering physical lethargy overcame my body. I thought I was going to die. I told my Spanish teacher I had a migraine and needed to go home. I made the unbelievably stupid and dangerous decision to drive home. I then lay down convinced that I wasn't going to wake up. By the grace of God, I did.

I had some anxiety issues and a problem with clenching my teeth at night. I was prescribed at various times some powerful benzodiazepines as a result, which I readily abused—Klonopin, Lorazepam, and Xanax—taking high doses straight up my nose.

I frequently got my hands on strong ADHD medications such as Adderall (a form of amphetamine), crushing and snorting the medication to get high. Cocaine was a thankfully short-lived experiment for me. Such substances were not to be found in the littler corner of the world I lived in, but were obtained in seedy locations in the Salt Lake valley area. The times I got a hold of it, it felt like a movie—being in situations and with people that may have actually been dangerous and volatile. I can see why cocaine is so destructive. It makes you feel like superman and is incredibly addictive. I once snorted lines of cocaine from the stainless-steel toilet paper cover of a truck stop bathroom in Green River, Utah (go ahead and look up where that is) while my parents were outside waiting for me to go. I was, I believe, sixteen or seventeen years old. So as much as I thought of myself as reasonable, I tended to be only slightly less reckless than the rest.

I think it was a great blessing for me that getting my hands on hard drugs was, for the most part, difficult while living in a small town. For those with means and easy access, hard drugs are a recipe for disaster. But persistence is all that is really required. Meth was the most accessible, as it was cooked by some people in town. I stayed away from it, as did some of my friends, but others in our group got sucked into its world. The stories could go on and on, maybe even fill an entire book themselves.

In tandem with the drug and alcohol abuse, I enveloped myself in punk rock music and the political and social counterculture it had to offer. My parents had given me an acoustic guitar when I was eleven and paid for lessons for a year. Near the end of that year, I started discovering punk rock music and began pouring hours a day into playing the guitar and listening to music—playing in a couple of bands over the years, one of which became a central focus of my life. Because of the rise of the internet, punk rock music and culture seemed immediately accessible even to a bunch of angsty teens in rural Utah where the politics were Republican and the music country.

The punk rock music scene—or what I could decipher of that scene from my corner of the world—introduced me to new, tantalizing, and radical ideas that spoke to me on a deep level, both emotionally and intellectually. I most certainly listened to and enjoyed my fair share of juvenile and vapid punk rock music, like Blink-182, but I gravitated almost instinctively to some of punk rock's headier themes, perhaps none more so than one of the most significant punk rock bands of all time, Bad Religion.

Besides Bad Religion's exceptional execution and mix of melodic and hard sounds, soaring vocals, and driving beats, it had something deeper: a message, exemplified perhaps no better than by the band's logo, a simple black Latin cross circled in red with a dash through it. To this day, Bad Religion's lyrics reflect, more often than not, serious and unusually thought-out themes and arguments in favor of scientific materialism. After all, the band's lead singer, Greg Graffin, had a Ph.D. in evolutionary biology, and when the band was not touring, he taught courses at UCLA. The lyrics of bands like Bad Religion and others, at least at the time, seemed to be probing serious questions and presenting answers that conflicted with what I had always been taught.

The God presented by Bad Religion was vindictive, morally obtuse, and capricious, as described in the song "Skyscraper", a stylized account of the Tower of Babel, in which God tears down the tower "like a spoiled little baby, who can't come out and play".[2] Similarly, the popular song "Sorrow", a meditation on the Book of Job, sharply criticizes God as portrayed in that famous account:

> Let me take you to the herding ground,
> Where all good men are trampled down;
> Just to settle a bet that could not be won,
> Between a prideful father and his son.[3]

They raised points that made me wonder about the morality of the God of the Bible, querying,

> I don't know what stopped Jesus Christ
> From turning every hungry stone into bread.
> And I don't remember hearing how Moses reacted
> When the innocent first born sons lay dead.
> Well, I guess God was a lot more demonstrative,
> Back when he flamboyantly parted the sea.
> Now everybody's praying
> Don't pray on me.[4]

But what would replace these theistic ideas of a backward pre-enlightenment age? The band's answer was the cold and nihilistic realities of scientific materialism, which they taught in catchy songs that would even quote eighteenth-century Scottish geologist James Hutton in their bleak picture of an unforgiving and deterministic universe with no free will or objective meaning.

[2] Brett Gurewitz, "Skyscraper", track 13 on Bad Religion, *Recipe for Hate*, Epitaph Records, 1993.

[3] Brett Gurewitz and Greg Graffin, "Sorrow", track 8 on Bad Religion, *The Process of Belief*, Epitaph Records, 2002.

[4] Brett Gurewitz, "Don't Pray on Me", track 11 on Bad Religion, *Recipe for Hate*, Epitaph Records, 1993.

During these years, I began to entertain quite seriously the idea that life was ultimately meaningless and that the existence of God was a noble lie we told ourselves to get through all the pointlessness. I don't mean to make myself into too much of a philosopher. A mix of fear (I found the idea of no longer existing after death horrifying) and apathy, with the ever-present alternative of "Who cares? Let's get wasted" to be an easy way to avoid taking life too seriously. But these ideas were always in the background of my life. Our group of friends, somewhat inebriated, would take to debating the meaning of life. It was a not-infrequent discussion among some of us. And it manifested itself in my band's songs, too. My lyrical stylings were not particularly good, but they reflected typical teenage angst and some of my own philosophical and religious musings. One song, my favorite, was called "Nothing", which I tried to write to be full of contradictions, to give the sense of the paradox modernity presents to us: we've built up so much, but because of the likelihood that there is no God, it is all completely meaningless.

Politically, I began to lean hard to the left, believing that a mix of Marxism and ever-increasing individual auton-omy would solve the world's problems. September 11 happened. The sense that the United States, which I took for granted as being in control, actually *wasn't*, and that maybe *nothing* was in control, was overwhelming. It fueled more drug and alcohol use and an instinctive distrust of authority and the current political regime. During the Iraq war, I took great pleasure in wearing my NOFX T-shirt to school with George W. Bush's face on it, emblazoned with the words "Not My President".

To offer a reason for why my life took the turn that it did during those years would ultimately be, for me, specula-tion. From a religious perspective, it is tempting to connect the causal dots between one sin and the next and the next. Yet that explanation seems somewhat lacking. Many teenagers dabble here and there with alcohol or a little pot and never go as deep as I went. And I also had *some* lingering sense of boundaries and levelheadedness that kept certain activities at bay (at least for the time being). Was it my doubts about Mormonism beginning to manifest early on? Perhaps, but I am skeptical of reinterpreting my life with a trajectory that is a little *too* perfectly headed away from Mormonism and toward Catholicism; after all, my doubts at the time were more about theism than Mormonism, and there was nothing in particular about Mormonism as compared to some other religion that bothered me. So it is not that I had some searing questions about Joseph Smith *per se*. Was it my parents' absence in my early teens while they took care of my younger brother during his severe illness? I genuinely think that my parents were good—not perfect, but they did the best they could. And laying blame on them seems a bit too Freudian, a bit too tidy, and, to be honest, simply not consistent with how I remember feeling at the time. Was it teenage rebellion that, reinforced by a like-minded peer group, just kept going too far? I honestly do not know. Maybe the answer is one of these things; maybe it's some of these things; maybe it's none of these things. I will let the reader judge.

Another question the reader may be asking, to which I *do* have an answer, is how I lived a life of such manifest contradiction—engaging in serious drug use and risky behavior while earning an Eagle Scout award. The answer: mostly through lying. I mean, *all* of our families were Mormon, more or less, and *none* of them wanted us drinking and doing drugs. So we all kept a strange, clandestine balance, hoping our worlds would not collide. Mine really only did once, but they hit hard.

My parents left town one weekend during my freshman year of high school. I had been sluffing school (that is Utah-speak for skipping class) *a lot* at that point. When they left town, I basically skipped an entire day or two of school. I was supposed to go out of town that Saturday morning with the football team for an away game. But instead, I threw a rager at my house Friday night and didn't go to the game. That whole night was a blur that started with beer and a bong and ended with me waking up the next morning and not going on the road trip and then telling my parents when they got back that I was sick. Well, the following Monday the school finally called my parents to report my staggering number of unexcused absences that quarter. And while my dad was collecting his thoughts about it for a few days, he came across a beer bottle left in my backyard, unopened. When they confronted me, my excuses were flimsy. But the whole incident only made me angrier. I felt that my parents were grand inquisitors, prying into *my* life when they had no right to do so, talking to me about God and the church. It was all a load of nonsense.

I wound up grounded for several months, forbidden from hanging out with any of my older friends. I began dating a good girl, and in a short period of time I had stopped using pornography and alcohol and was seriously entertaining the idea of straightening things out in my life. But Mormon kids are not supposed to date before the age of sixteen, at least not exclusively. My parents would not bend, and ultimately, we had to break up. That was it for me. The one thing in my life that had, in fact, started to get me to behave the way my parents wanted was over. So internally, I surmised that they had no idea what they were doing, and, in abject anger, I swore that if it came from them, it was manifestly not worth listening to. Once the grounding was over, I just found more and more discreet ways of doing what I wanted to do—my drug and alcohol use increased, as did the porn—and I spent the rest of high school acquiring the unsavory anecdotes I divulged at the beginning of this chapter (and a good deal more than that) and plotting my way out of Mormonism, a course whose final destination lay somewhere beyond the horizon of high school and moving out.

I COULDN'T THINK STRAIGHT as I sat through the lesson that day. I don't remember what any of it was about. My entire recollection is like a scene from a Charlie Brown classroom: *Wah-wah-wah, wah-wah, wah-wah-wah-wah.* I had a small paper note in my hand on which I had written, "Bishop, can we talk after the meeting?" One of the key roles of Mormon bishops is to oversee and help shape the young men in the ward who are between the ages of sixteen and eighteen—the priests—and help them prepare to become "elders" and then to go serve a mission. I had never spoken with my bishop about what my life was really like. So, with more moral courage than I had probably ever mustered in my seventeen years of life, I slipped the note to him as he sat next to me in class that day. He read it and gave me a reassuring nod.

I cannot identify any single factor that pushed me to that point. At the time, there was a distinct and growing sense that things were coming to a head. Everyone in my band wanted us to "make it", to start touring and try our hand at being professional punk rockers. That was our dream. We spent hours practicing every day. To make things happen, we all knew that as soon as we finished high school, we needed to move to Salt Lake City or even somewhere else and start dedicating more time to our music. But as we grew older, tensions in the band

and in our broader circle of friends were forming, and
more important still, our reckless lifestyles were catching
up with us and imposing consequences on us. Drugs were
an increasingly central feature of our days, which meant a
proportionately increasing risk of run-ins with the law. I
don't think I will ever forget the feeling that swept over
me when I heard the news that a group of our friends,
including two members of the band, had been "busted"—
and I don't mean by their parents. There was a fairly large
amount of marijuana involved (over a pound), which
meant this time it was serious. Possession with intent to
distribute, at least, and someone was going to county for
sure, but possibly to the Point of the Mountain—the state
prison. One close friend, who had just found out that
his girlfriend was pregnant, understandably informed on
another close friend. Things got ugly among the whole
group. One by one, these sorts of thing started happening
to our group of friends. I was still at the periphery of the
local police's scrutiny, and it seemed clear that unless I
veered hard in the opposite direction, things were not
going to work out for me.

Moreover, given all of this, I began to ask myself
whether we were really going to get our band signed by a
record label and start touring and make a living that way.
We were all right for a group of eighteen-to-twenty-year-
olds, but let's just say we weren't obviously destined for
greatness. At one point, some of our friends had moved
out of Blanding and were living in an apartment in American Fork, Utah. I visited them once and got a glimpse
of the future. The place was a dump—a two-bedroom
basement apartment that looked like the crew of *Jackass*
lived there. The horribly stained carpet was barely visible
beneath untold layers of empty beer cans and Little Caesars
pizza boxes. Mattresses on the floor. Burt was sleeping in

a closet. The place reeked of stale tobacco, pot, and BO. They all thought it was awesome. Pondering all of this, it struck me that rather than our band "making it", it was at least as likely, and looking increasingly more so, that we'd give it a shot, struggle, live in some such dumpy apartment, keep doing drugs, and wind up burned-out losers who returned to Blanding to become the next generation of Ricks, buying booze for high school kids. And sure enough, my friends who moved away while I was still in high school could never seem to keep their life together. They all eventually wound up right back in Blanding. I didn't want to be Rick.

At the same time, the closer I got to age eighteen, the closer I was to age nineteen, which meant the closer I was to having to decide whether I would go on a Mormon mission. From my early or mid-teens, I was clearly decided *against* going on a mission, because I didn't want to be Mormon. But there was obviously some not-insignificant pressure to do so. My father had been a missionary in North Carolina, Virginia, and West Virginia when he was nineteen. My oldest brother served in Chicago, the next in Bogotá, Columbia, the next in Guatemala City. I looked up to all of them. They had been missionaries, come home, gotten married, and started families and were happy. Happy like my mom and dad and like our family had been growing up. The good influences in my life were always there in the background. I would sit in seminary and think, *What if this is true?* I participated in those classes and even enjoyed them from time to time, because I liked to ponder questions about God. To the everlasting credit of the good Mormon kids in my town, when I started creeping into their social circles in order to distance myself a bit from my other friends, they never rejected my advances. They welcomed me in. And one day, all these forces and pressures converged, and I decided to do the unthinkable—go to the bishop, confess what kind of life I had been up to, and stop, with the hope that I might go and be a missionary.

Confession is not a regular thing in the Mormon faith. That is to say, unlike the Catholic faith, where penance is a sacrament to be partaken of regularly, "confession" in the Mormon Church is reserved for only "serious" sins— sexual transgression or violating the Word of Wisdom, for instance. Every year, starting around age twelve, we had "worthiness" interviews in which, at the time, we met privately with the bishop, who would ask a series of set questions about our spiritual development, our testimony of Joseph Smith and the *Book of Mormon*, and whether we had sins we needed to confess. I had been through many such interviews over the years, and I had lied my way through just about all of them. But the time had come for me to make a choice, and I chose the Mormon faith. Really, there was not much else for me to choose. It was all I knew and all I possibly could have known, given the time and circumstances.

Bishop Ron Kirk was a good man. Everyone left after class and headed home; we met in his office and he asked, "What do you want to talk about, Jeremy?" And then I broke down. The catharsis was real and resulted in a deep emotional outpouring. For years, I had been using pornography regularly, pushing the line with girls too far, drinking, doing drugs, and not living the way I was supposed to live as a Mormon, but I wanted to change because I wanted to serve a mission. And so I had come to him to confess and get my life in order. He gave me some good counsel and said he would be available twenty-four hours a day. If I ever felt like I was going to give in to a temptation to do anything I shouldn't do, he said to just give him a call and he would drop whatever he was doing to help me through it. He was a good man.

It felt good. It felt right. How could it not? To own up to sin with some real sorrow relieves the soul. And it did mine. But real change doesn't happen overnight. My reversion to Mormonism had fits and starts, some missteps and mistakes, and some returns of demons. But I was overcoming by doing what I had been told my whole life to do: pray, read the *Book of Mormon*, learn about the Mormon faith, and try to live it. Be with good people. Do good things. Try to gain a testimony.

One night during my senior year in high school changed things. Although I had consciously decided to leave the old life, I was struggling to get out. I set a certain date after which I would be done with it all. I told myself, "This will be the last time, the last hurrah." But I knew I shouldn't do it. Planning a last hurrah hardly seemed like I was really sorry for the life I had been living. But I gave in to habit rather than going with what was plainly the correct choice. It actually was the last time I ever used illegal drugs, but it didn't go as planned.

One of my friends had purchased some psychedelic mushrooms, and I got some and took them. I went over to another friend's house where we were all meeting up for the trip. But immediately, something happened that had not happened in a long time: my conscience spoke—loudly—and I knew that this experience was not going to be what I had planned on. *This is wrong. What you are doing is wrong. You know what you are doing is wrong.* I began to grow increasingly introspective, and about the time I could feel that the mushrooms were actually kicking in, which intensified the introspection, I told my friends on the other side of the room: "Someone take me home."

"You are just having a bad trip. Relax and it will go away."

I was insistent. "I don't give a shit. Take me home." So they did. I went downstairs, went to my room, closed the door, and spent a long night thinking about my life, about God, where I wanted my life to go, and what choices I would make. After many hours, I went up to my parents' room in the middle of the night, woke them up, and told them I was making a change in my life. I came clean about basically everything I had been up to—much of which they suspected, some of which they knew, and some of which was probably a shock. My dad could tell I was not totally with it. My life demonstrably changed from that moment on. You can call it whatever you like, but it marked a change in me. Still, I did not have a "testimony" of the *Book of Mormon*. And I was aware of that.

I made a clean break with my old friends, something they noticed and that invariably blighted almost all of those relationships. I began to devote massive amounts of time to preparing to become a missionary. I read the entire *Book of Mormon*. I read much of the Bible. I devoured official Mormon theology and literature and the history of Joseph Smith. I read the six-hundred-page book by Elder James E. Talmage, *Jesus the Christ*—a systematic theology of Mormon belief—in a week. The more I dove into the church's materials, and the more I began wanting to believe it was true, the more my life seemed at peace and the more sorrow I began to feel over the life I had lived. When I had initially gone to the bishop, I'm not sure I was really sorry; I was mostly just doing what I was supposed to do. But I began to feel real sorrow for my sins and to start to question sincerely whether I could ever truly be prepared to go out into the world and be a missionary, preaching Christ's true Restored Gospel to the world. Racked with anxiety on June 27, 2005, sitting on my bed in a state of deep mental and spiritual distress, I opened up the *Book of Mormon* randomly and read a passage that seemed like its words were penned for that very moment. They were exactly what I needed to hear:

> And this is the means whereby salvation cometh. And there is none other salvation save this which hath been spoken of; neither are there any conditions whereby man can be saved except the conditions which I have told you.
>
> Believe in God; believe that he is, and that he created all things, both in heaven and in earth; believe that he has all wisdom, and all power, both in heaven and in earth; believe that man doth not comprehend all the things which the Lord can comprehend. (Mosiah 4:8–9)

I was sobbing. But I felt an overwhelming sense of rightness, in my life—that everything would be okay—but also as to what I was reading. God himself had answered the deepest troubles of my heart, telling me by both the burning in my bosom and the enlightenment in my mind. This was it. The Holy Ghost had spoken to me. This is what everyone had been talking about, teaching me about, promising me would happen. It was all true! *This* was a testimony. Now I *knew*.

My growing sense of purpose was amplified when I received what is known as a patriarchal blessing. This is a religious, prophetic ceremony in which a special Mormon priesthood leader called a patriarch places his hands on someone's head after deep spiritual preparation and pronounces a special prophetic blessing about that person's life. Mormons often refer to this as personal scripture. The two purposes of this blessing are to declare which of the twelve tribes of Israel you belong to (Mormons believe in a gathering-of-Israel theology in which we all belong to one of the twelve tribes) and to provide a prophetic blue-print for your life. It is something to which you can return over and over again when you are seeking to find answers to difficult problems. It served for me as a ready source of comfort for years to come.

The patriarch's wife usually sits in and records the bless-ing on a tape recorder or some other device and then tran-scribes it. You are given a copy, and a copy is sent to the Mormon Church's headquarters, where it is kept on file and can be retrieved in the future if you lose your copy. On July 17, 2005, I received mine, which read as follows:

Brother Jeremy Max Christiansen, as an ordained Patri-arch in the Melchizedek Priesthood I lay my hands upon your head and pronounce your patriarchal blessing; a blessing that comes from your Father in Heaven and that is intended as a guidel [sic] and is intended to provide direction for your life.

Your lineage is through the loins of Ephraim and the Lord expects you to live the gospel fully and to provide a proper example for those around you.

Your life is one of service. The Lord has blessed you with many talents and as you live develop those talents, keep in mind the purpose for which you are blessed. Use them to build up the kingdom of our Father in Heaven and to bless lives.

You will be led, as you live worthy of our Father in Heaven's direction, to find your eternal companion. You will go with her to the temple and there be sealed. You will raise up a righteous seed unto our Father in Heaven. As the patriarch of your family, you will be led and directed by the Holy Ghost in the things that you are to do.

As you listen to the still, small voice and as you apply it's [sic] promptings, your life will be of meaningful ser-vice. Your success in life will allow you to accomplish the things our Father in Heaven has sent you here to do.

Your parents have given you direction in living the gospel. As you apply their teachings, you will be blessed. As you, in turn, set the example and apply those principles in your own life, your family, too, will be blessed.

Your Heavenly Father is pleased with the good things that you do and He will continue to direct your life and help you develop the talents and abilities and gifts that have been given to you.

Your gift is one of blessing lives by helping others feel good about themselves. Remember always that your attitude towards others will help them determine the way that they feel about themselves. As you use this gift to treat others with kindness and respect, your life will be blessed and you will be a blessing to others.

Your Father in Heaven loves you and will direct your paths. He will direct you through the scriptures as you study and as you listen to His still, small voice.

To this end I bless, you, in the name of Jesus Christ, amen.

With time and experience, I came to see something unique about my blessing (whether it really was unique, I do not know): its sparseness. For instance, my wife's patriarchal blessing contains several single-spaced pages. Mission companions would later tell me, too, that their blessings were much longer. Patriarchal blessings are not meant to be shared with people other than your parents, maybe, and your spouse. But as a missionary, when I told someone my patriarchal blessing was unusually short, he asked to see it from a distance. I pulled it out, and he could see it almost fit on a single sheet of paper, double-spaced, only going a couple of lines onto the back of the page. He agreed, surprised, that it was significantly shorter than his. I fretted over this, for some reason, at different points in my life, but my dad gave me some advice. He said,

"God has told you what's right and what you need to do, and he trusts you to go do it; you don't need a bunch of specifics." This advice, along with my patriarchal blessing, helped infuse my life with a deep sense of purpose and a deep desire to stay in tune with God so that I could try as best as I could to do always what he wanted me to do—to be always worthy to receive revelation from God about what to do in my life.

The next step in my path was to be ordained an elder in the church and to receive the Melchizedek priesthood. It was an emotional event for my parents, who were seeing their son transform before their eyes in such a short period of time. When Mormon men receive the Melchizedek priesthood and are ordained to some office in that priesthood (such as elder), it is customary for the man doing the ordaining to present a line of authority to you. It is a genealogy, tracing that man's ordination to the priesthood back—link by link, name by name—to Jesus Christ himself. My father was ordained by Fred Eugene Halliday, who was ordained by Arlow L. Freestone, who was ordained by Theodore M. Burton, who was ordained by Marion G. Romney, who was ordained by Joseph Fielding Smith, who was ordained by Joseph F. Smith, who was ordained by Brigham Young, who was ordained by Oliver Cowdery, Martin Harris, and David Whitmer, who were ordained by Joseph Smith Jr., who was ordained by Peter, James, and John, who were ordained by Jesus Christ.

It was an emotional experience. I wrote in my journal that day, July 30, 2005:

Today after church I was ordained an elder and received the Melchizedek Priesthood from my father, Mark W. Christiansen.... It was very spiritual. My dad gave an address to me at the beginning of the night regarding my line of authority. As he read back the names [in the line] they began to be very familiar and famous. As he said, "Joseph Smith, who [was] ordained at the hands of Peter, James, and John, on the banks of the Susquehanna River," a very powerful feeling came to me.... I could not physically stop myself from crying, although I tried.

I knew, by the power of the Holy Ghost, that I had received the priesthood that Jesus Christ gave to his apostles, and that those apostles had given to Joseph Smith, just as I had been taught. That same feeling overwhelmed me. And such experiences would continue as a regular part of my life. As I learned more about my faith and strove earnestly to practice it, it seemed God was confirming to me that it was all true. I spent hours in a small room in my parents' basement, where I was living just prior to leaving on my mission, listening to CDs of a lengthy set of lectures by a Brigham Young University professor named Truman Madsen, in which he recounted numerous historical accounts of the life of Joseph Smith. They showed him to be, while not perfect, a man of impeccable character. I remember Professor Madsen quoting Joseph Smith, stating, "No one can ever enter the celestial kingdom unless he is strictly honest." Those words struck me, as I had developed such a habit of deceit in my youth. I committed to being honest, just like Joseph Smith. The Prophet became my hero. My heart swelled listening to those lectures.

Around this time, I submitted papers to become a missionary for the church and was waiting for the letter to come back from the president of the Mormon Church, assigning me to a mission somewhere in the world. I recorded in my journal that I had had a "distinct impression upon my brain" and felt "very compelled that I am going to Cochabamba, Bolivia" on my mission. I noted that Brother Draper, my mission preparation course teacher, "said he felt that he was going to be a Mission President so distinctly" before it happened, and that "he wrote it down but feared" he was being "pretentious" or "prideful", but he went ahead and recorded the impression anyway. Inspired by his example, I went out on a limb and did the same, because the way he "described [his] impression" was "like it is for me".

Before I could go on a mission, there was another crucial step—I had to receive my Temple Endowment. Mormon theology focuses on various "ordinances of salvation", ceremonies necessary to be saved, somewhat like the idea of the sacraments in the Catholic Church, though with important differences. Baptism is an ordinance. The Lord's Supper is an ordinance. Receiving the priesthood, for men, is an ordinance. And all of these ordinances come with an associated covenant or covenants, promises Mormons make to God with blessings in return from God. The highest, holiest, and most sacred of these are the ordinances performed in Mormon temples. Mormons do not speak about them outside of the temple because they are sacred. Indeed, the covenants one makes in the temple include the commitment not to disclose certain aspects of those ceremonies. I recount here only what is necessary to my story, although I assume some Mormons will be uncomfortable with what I discuss, while others will think it appropriately circumscribed. This isn't an exposé. My purpose is to explain my growing, all-encompassing commitment to Mormonism and the reasons for it.

It is not uncommon for Mormon parents, just before their children go to the temple to receive their Endowments, to sit them down and sort of prepare them for what they are about to experience. Mormon Sunday services are more in the vein of "low church" Evangelical Protestantism: no pomp, no ceremony. The temple is so much a departure from that low-church style of worship, and the ceremony frankly so cryptic and different, that it catches many Mormons off guard and, at least the first time, can be an unpleasant experience. One of my aunts went to the temple and was sealed to her husband, and they never returned and quickly became inactive in the church. On the twenty-minute drive to Monticello, my dad and I rode alone. He told me that I might be tempted to freak out a little—that this might look like some weird conspiracy or secret society. But he assured me it was all sacred and beautiful, and that in time, I would come to see it that way too. There was deep symbolism from which I would learn in the temple about God's purpose for my life and his Plan of Salvation for mankind.

I arrived at the temple on November 26, 2005, dressed in ordinary Sunday clothes (a white shirt and tie) but carrying a side bag that contained white pants, shoes, and socks, and also a white satchel inside of which were white ceremonial robes and a sash, white cap, and Kelly-green apron with fig-leaf designs embroidered on it that together comprise the ceremonial clothing for Mormon temples. On that day, I would go through two temple ordinances for myself: the Washing and Anointing and the Endowment (in the future, I would go to the temple many times to receive the ordinances as a proxy for someone who had died but whose genealogy a member of the church had completed).

After a brief visit with the temple president, I was escorted to a locker room where I was instructed to take off all my clothes and underwear and put on a white robe. I then went toward a small complex of white curtains set up to make four small "rooms". I was seated on a chair when a temple ordinance worker, wearing a white suit and tie, came in and began the ordinance of Washing and Anointing. After a brief explanation of the ordinance, connecting it with the washing and anointing of Aaron in the Book of Exodus, he called me by my full name and told me that through his priesthood authority he was washing me, preparatory to my receiving my anointings, that I might become "clean from the blood and sins of this generation". He dipped his finger in a small vat of water and rubbed it with his thumb across my forehead, then began an extended blessing ritual in which he pronounced that all parts of my body—my head, brain, ears, eyes, nose, lips, neck, shoulders, back, breast, vitals, bowels, arms, hands, loins, legs, and feet—were washed, each with an attendant spiritual blessing. For example, my ears were washed that I would hear the word of the Lord, my eyes that I might see clearly and discern between truth and error, and my arms and hands that they might be strong and wield the sword of justice in defense of truth and virtue. From behind the next curtained room, another temple worker appeared and placed his hands on my head, which "sealed" the washing.

I was then escorted to the next curtained room, where the second temple worker took a small amount of olive oil and poured it on top of my head, anointing me preparatory to becoming a king and a priest unto the Most High God, to rule and reign in the house of Israel forever. He then placed his hands on my hand and repeated the same litany I had heard in the previous room, and another worker came in and "sealed" the anointing "through [my] faithfulness". I pondered deeply on all of this. Just as my patriarchal blessing, all of these blessings were contingent on my faithfulness to Christ. I felt a deep commitment to the church through that ritual, which I would repeat many times in my life and which always felt like a beautiful spiritual boon.

I then passed to the next room, where the officiator gave me the temple garment, worn by faithful Mormons as underclothing, instructing me to wear it throughout my life. I was taught that it was a symbolic piece of clothing, representing the garment given to Adam and Even when they were found naked in the Garden—a symbol of God's love and protection for me. I was promised, again contingent on my faith, that as long as I honored my covenants made in the temple, the garment would be a shield and a protection to me until my time on Earth was finished. I found that to be a beautiful sentiment of God's paternal care for me, and felt that through seeking to do his will, I could always be assured that I would be able to fulfill my mission, whatever it might be, here in mortality. The worker then bestowed on me a "new name" which I was to "keep sacred and never reveal" except during a certain portion of the temple ceremony. My new name was Lazarus, which profoundly impacted me. It was especially fitting, because Christ had, in a sense, raised me from the dead life I had been living to a new one in him.

From there I dressed in my white shirt, tie, pants, and shoes, took my satchel of temple robes, and was seated in the room for the Endowment ceremony. The Endowment is a religious ritual in which participants are taken through a dramatized representation of God's Plan of Salvation, focused on the Creation and the events in the Garden of Eden and shortly thereafter. While in some temples the Endowment is acted out by live volunteer actors, the Monticello temple, like most, had a large screen where much of the Endowment is played as a film, with various pauses in the film where the participants take part in important religious rituals.

As the ceremony began, we were instructed that during the Endowment, each of us would make certain promises that were sacred and guarded by a solemn covenant made in the presence of God, angels, and witnesses, and that the violation of those covenants would bring upon us God's judgment. The officiator also told us that if there was anyone present who of his own free will and choice wished not to proceed, he could raise his hand and be escorted out.

The lights dimmed, and the dramatized movie began, presenting the story of Creation with the voices of and references to three persons: Elohim, Jehovah, and Michael. Elohim repeatedly sends Jehovah and Michael down to perform the various tasks on the six days of Creation, with Jehovah and Michael returning to report after each day. On the sixth day, Elohim observes that man is not on the Earth, and they decide to all go down to put him there. Elohim and Jehovah create a body for Michael, who is then renamed Adam and caused to forget his previous life in the heavens. From there, they create Eve. The story progresses more or less as the Bible narrates, with the exception of the appearance of Satan, who is not portrayed as a serpent but as an ostentatiously dressed man.

A gnawing sense of confusion arose in me over how the Fall of Adam and Eve was presented. It seemed self-contradictory to me, because Elohim commanded Adam and Eve to have children—something Adam and Eve were not capable of doing at that time according to our beliefs, since they were innocent like children and had no sexual desire—and then forbade them from eating of the Tree of the Knowledge of Good and Evil, which would, among other things, make them capable of having children. In the ceremonial dialogue, Adam and Eve teach that it was necessary for them to disobey God's command regarding the Tree of the Knowledge of Good and Evil in order for them to keep his commandment of multiplying and replenishing the Earth. It was something that "must needs be", and it was "better" for them to fall so that they could "know the good from the evil" rather than stay in the Garden. Yet, of course God punishes them for disobeying him and imposes the traditional biblical curses upon them (Eve will bear her children in sorrow and Adam will be forced to eat by the sweat of his brow). Furthermore, when God is chastising Adam and Eve for this disobedience, he calls Satan out from hiding to punish him as well. God asks him what he has been doing, and his reply is that he has "been giving some of the fruit of the tree of the knowledge of good and evil to" Adam and Eve, "*the same as it has been done in other worlds*". My mind absolutely raced at this line. What could that possibly mean? God curses Satan with the traditional biblical curse ("on thy belly shalt thou go"), and Satan cries foul, raising his fist at God and warning that if God curses him for doing "the same thing that has been done in other worlds", he will take the spirits that followed him out of heaven and wage war on Earth against Adam and Eve's descendants. The presentation did not shake me or cause me doubts, but rather, I was genuinely confused over why it seemed that God presented Adam and Eve with a commandment impossible to keep, commanded them not to do the one thing that would enable them to keep that commandment, and then cursed them when they broke the latter commandment to keep the former—all of which was necessary for God's remaining spirit children to come to Earth. And Satan's remark about this process having been used in other worlds (but apparently not authorized for this one) was beyond mysterious to me. But I ultimately took it all to be part of the deeper, sacred, symbolic meaning of the temple that would become clearer to me through ongoing revelation throughout my life and regular temple attendance and participation. I trusted. And with time, temple worship appealed to me greatly and brought me interior peace for many years.

After casting Adam and Eve out of the Garden, God continues his plan by sending messengers from heaven, the pre-mortal apostles Peter, James, and John, to cast the continuously badgering Satan out of Adam and Eve's presence and to teach them progressively more and more about how to make it back to God's presence. Specifically, they present Adam and Eve with God's laws, and with each law and covenant, they offer an associated sign and token—that is, a signal made with the hands and a hand clasp. The sacred names of the signs and tokens, as well as the signs and tokens themselves, were never to be revealed except during certain parts of the temple ceremony and were the key to entering God's presence at the end of our lives. Whether this was meant literally or, perhaps more likely to my mind, symbolically was never entirely clear to me. As a teenager, I had already read on the internet that there were parallels between the ceremonies of Freemasonry and the Mormon Endowment, including the signs and tokens and much other temple symbolism. But trusting in the writings of people such as Mormon professor Dr. Hugh Nibley, I firmly believed that the Endowment ceremony was ancient, whatever the specific vehicle may have been through which Joseph Smith chose to reveal these sacred truths.

During the ceremony that day, I made several covenants to live a life dedicated to God. The promises were straightforward commitments to live a Christian life, including being obedient to God in all things; being willing to sacrifice everything I had—even my life if necessary—in sustaining and defending his kingdom; being chaste; "avoid[ing] ... evil speaking of the Lord's anointed" (church leaders); adjuring all "unholy and impure practice[s]"; and finally, consecrating all my time, talents, and everything the Lord had given to me or would later give to me to the church. In a nutshell, I covenanted to be faithful to God in all things he commanded. At the end of each distinct covenant, we were asked to bow our heads and say yes in affirmation that we promised and covenanted to live these laws. I fervently said yes to each of them.

The temple was filled with symbolism from top to bottom. Typically, during each progressive phase of the Endowment, participants moved from one room to another and then to another. The physical movement—in larger temples, often going up stairs between rooms—symbolically pointed to the upward journey to heaven that could be achieved by keeping our covenants. In the second-to-last room, at the head of the room beyond the altar, there was a great, lavish Victorian-style curtain. The curtain was raised up, and behind it was "the veil of the temple": a series of large white curtains with the "marks of the Holy Priesthood" embroidered on them at little stations where people could stand in front of them, with openings in the veil cut in the shape of those same marks so you could reach through the holes. The veil separated the Celestial Room, which represented the highest degree of heaven, where God resides, from the rest of the temple. To me, it was as if it suggested the thinness of the separation between man and God. As the Mormon children's primary song went,

> Heavenly Father, are you really there?
> And do you hear and answer ev'ry child's prayer?
> Some say that heaven is far away,
> But I feel it close around me as I pray.[5]

[5] "A Child's Prayer", in *Children's Songbook*, ed. The Church of Jesus Christ of Latter-day Saints (Salt Lake City: Church of Jesus Christ of Latter-day Saints, 1989), 12.

This great veil, which was opaque but only barely so, seemed to be a representation of just how close God is to us, or how close we could be to him if we so chose.

The meaning of each of the marks—the square, compass, navel, and knee marks, also embroidered on the garments given to me to wear outside the temple under my clothing—was explained. Again, I was aware that those marks were borrowed from Freemasonry, but their meanings in the Endowment were different. Each one served as a reminder of the covenants made in the temple, a physical token worn at all times to help me remember my dependence on Jesus Christ and God's Word.

In the final portion of the Endowment, Adam and Eve are to be presented at the veil. They have been taught all of God's laws, and the time has come for them to return to God's presence. Each person in the ceremony then goes up, one by one, and at the veil engages in a small ritual dialogue with a person on the other side who tests the participant's knowledge of the signs and tokens of the priesthood. I was told that I would be going last—that is, all of my family members who were there, along with everyone else, would go through first. I was nervous and struggling to remember all the various names and key words and phrases associated with the different hand clasps. A kind old man was there at the veil to help me through it. After the ritual dialogue was over, the temple worker on the other side, who represents God in the dialogue, said, "Let him enter."

With that, the person on the other side pulled me through the veil and ushered me into the Celestial Room, where all of my family were waiting for me. My mother, weeping with joy, rushed over to hug me. I wept. My dad joined. It was an overwhelming spiritual and emotional experience, punctuated by the beautiful tradition of having all of one's attendant family members pass through first, so that as you symbolically pass from life into eternity, you find yourself in a majestic, opulent, beautiful, and serene room where your family awaits you. This was heaven. This was what heaven was. This was what the Gospel of Jesus Christ was about. This is what I wanted everyone on my mission to receive. This was the goal. This was all that mattered. I wrote in my journal that day:

> Today I received my endowment in the Monticello, Utah temple, in the 12 Noon session. It was different. Although I don't fully understand everything and I doubt that I ever will, I received a calm assuran[t] witness of the Spirit that it is of God, it is the truth, and it is a necessary ordinance that will allow me, if I will be true and faithful, to again walk back into the presence of Christ and my Father in Heaven. The temple is the Gospel of Jesus Christ. It is special, it is sacred, and it is true, and I know, for the Spirit has told it to my soul. Although it is very different, I have an assurance it's right.

Three days later, November 29, 2005, I recorded, "Today I received my mission call to the Argentina Buenos Aires North Mission. I am very humbled by this experience." Of course, I realized that my impression about Bolivia had not been accurate. And I wrote, "I may have been over pretentious in expecting to go to another place, so it must have been just me." But I continued, "I am so thankful for this opportunity to serve the Lord. I am thankful for the opportunity to make amends for my mistakes by serving the Lord, and I hope to do it with all my heart, might, mind, and strength. I will report to the [Missionary Training Center] in Provo, Utah, on February 8, 2006." Understanding that I was still learning and lacked the spiritual insight and preparedness to discern God's will accurately as I was being taught by those around me, I was nonetheless ready to preach the Gospel to the world, hopeful that God would help me do my best.

3

I Hope They Call Me on a Mission

I hope they call me on a mission
When I have grown a foot or two.
I hope by then I will be ready
To teach and preach and work as missionaries do.
I hope that I can share the gospel
With those who want to know the truth.
I want to be a missionary
And serve and help the Lord while I am in my youth.[1]

I'VE KNOWN THAT MORMON children's song as long as I can remember, and the time came for me to do like my dad did and all my older brothers had done—go preach the Gospel.

When I was a missionary, everyone pretty much acknowledged that the drop-off at the Missionary Training Center (MTC for short) was emotionally brutalizing. I don't mean that in a critical way. We all just sort of laughed at how gut-wrenching the scene tends to be. It is a more organized version of the early scene in the Audrey Hepburn classic *The Nun's Story* where her father drops her off and says his final goodbyes before she becomes a cloistered nun.

[1] "I Hope They Call Me on a Mission", in *Children's Songbook*, ed. The Church of Jesus Christ of Latter-day Saints (Salt Lake City: Church of Jesus Christ of Latter-day Saints, 1989), 169.

I would spend eight weeks there for language instruction and training in proselytizing. My family brought me to the MTC, there was some initial checking in and paperwork, and then everyone was ushered into a large room with a raised pulpit at the front and a large projector screen. There was the opening song "Called to Serve", a prayer, and then a speech by the president of the MTC. After that, they put on a short emotional documentary-style movie about the moment after you walk out of that room and leave your family and what will happen over the next few weeks. It really primes the waterworks. And when it was over, basically everyone was sobbing because they knew what came next. We stood up, and the MTC president said for everyone to say their goodbyes and that it was time for the missionaries to leave through the doors on the right and the families to leave on the left. I had a lump in my throat. My parents cried. They told me how proud they were that I had changed my life and made it this far. Then we parted.

Missionary life is rigorous. There are rules—strict rules—and you are expected to obey them. You are assigned a companion, and you never leave his side except to go to the bathroom. A million horror stories (half-legend, half-true) are told and retold of good, well-meaning missionaries leaving their companions alone for just a bit, just a moment, and *boom*, just like that, the next thing you know they are breaking the law of chastity with some girl, causing immense scandal to the work in that area for untold decades, getting sent home in disgrace, and probably being excommunicated from the church. You get up at 6:30 A.M and go to bed at 10:30 P.M. every day. No TV. No movies (except church films). "Exact obedience" is a phrase repeated over and over. This all makes complete sense, to be honest. An army of 50,000-plus nineteen-year-old boys with the Mormon Church's reputation to spoil out there could be a complete disaster if things were not run as a pretty tight ship. So the rules were strict, and I worked hard to keep them exactly. I never wanted to do anything that would bring my family embarrassment. To make them proud was a constant motivation for me.

Life in the MTC for someone like me who would be going to another country was primarily about acquiring language skills—hours and hours a day spent learning Spanish. We followed a program called Speak Your Language: if you know a word in your language, don't say it in English anymore. My journals, which I have normalized for the purposes of this book, were, in those early days, filled to the brim with an increasingly Spanglish prose, reflecting my sincere desire to learn the language. I had taken Spanish in high school, so I knew a fair amount of the basics. I was moved out of beginning language and into the intermediate level on my first or second full day, where the language training was a bit more advanced.

The other main purpose of the MTC is to prepare you to teach the message of the "Restoration of the Gospel". At the time, this was done through a systematized and boiled-down series of brief lessons (that can be presented flexibly, according to people's perceived needs) about the Mormon message, all aggressively geared toward getting prospective converts to read the *Book of Mormon* and to pray about it and the other claims of Mormonism so that they, too, can have that witness from the Holy Ghost, join the church, receive the saving ordinances, and, hopefully, through perseverance to the end in the faith, go to God's Celestial Kingdom. Thus, the notion of "feeling the Spirit"—that testimonial experience—permeates everything at the MTC and is a massive component of the training in missionary life and a focus of day-to-day pros-elytizing in the field.

As chapter 4 of the official Mormon missionary train-ing manual, *Preach My Gospel*, instructed me, "You will succeed in your work as you learn to receive and follow personal revelation.... [God] will help you as you try to recognize and understand the Spirit." I was instructed "to seek and receive personal revelation through the Holy Ghost as you help people become baptized and con-firmed". The church encouraged me, "Have faith that you will receive personal revelation to guide you from day to day" and assured me, "The Holy Ghost will help you in every aspect of your work."[2]

My job was to help other people *feel* what I *felt*. I knew, just as *Preach My Gospel* instructed, that "the power of the Holy Ghost is central to conversion." But I had to learn "to understand ... the *experience* of conversion",[3] which, according to apostle Boyd K. Packer, required that "we ... understand what [a person] must *feel* in order to receive conversion."[4] As apostle M. Russell Ballard taught, "True conversion comes through the power of the Spirit.... When individuals ... *feel* the Spirit work-ing within them, or when they see the evidence of the Lord's love and mercy in their lives, they are edified and strengthened spiritually and their faith in Him increases. This is how we come to *feel* the gospel is true."[5]

[2] *Preach My Gospel: A Guide to Missionary Service* (Salt Lake City: Church of Jesus Christ of Latter-day Saints, 2019), chap. 4.

[3] *Preach My Gospel*, chap. 4.

[4] Elder Boyd K. Packer, "By the Spirit of the Truth", in *Teaching Seminary: Preservice Readings* (Salt Lake City: Church of Jesus Christ of Latter-day Saints, 2004).

[5] M. Russell Ballard, "Now Is the Time" (170th Annual General Conference of the Church of Jesus Christ of Latter-day Saints, Salt Lake City, Saturday Afternoon Session, April 5, 2000), *Ensign*, May 2008, https://www.churchof jesuschrist.org/study/general-conference/2000/10/now-is-the-time?lang=eng.

Thus, when I taught potential converts about prayer, *Preach My Gospel* instructed that God would respond through our *feelings*: "We must learn to listen to the still, small voice of the Spirit. We can recognize when the Holy Ghost is teaching us the truth. Our minds will be filled with inspiring and uplifting thoughts. We will be enlightened, or given new knowledge. Our hearts will have feelings of peace, joy, and love. We will want to do good and be helpful to others. These feelings are hard to describe but can be recognized as we experience them."[6]

My conversion to Mormonism deepened day by day according to this standard, as revealed in my journal entries:

- February 10, 2006: "The Spirit bore witness to me as I left [my family] that this is the right thing."
- February 10, 2006: "The Spirit was so strong." "I felt the Spirit so much."
- February 15, 2006: "I felt the Spirit very strongly."
- February 19, 2006: "[T]he Spirit was just so strong.... The Spirit bore witness to me that Joseph Smith really was a prophet, [he] is one of my heroes."
- February 26, 2006: "I can't explain the Spirit that was felt."

There are hundreds of such references in my missionary journals, consistently spanning the two years. And my reaction to those who challenged my knowledge was equally vehement. While I was in the MTC, we spent some time in a sort of evangelizing call center phoning people who had come to a Mormon visitor center and filled out a card wanting to know more and attempting to arrange for missionaries to go visit them. We called it the RC, the referral center. On February 18, 2006, I recorded:

[6] *Preach My Gospel*, chap. 4.

Today in the RC I felt some very powerful feelings & learned some very important lessons. Always have humility & teach by the Spirit. I also felt in some degree, I'm not saying I know, what Joseph Smith felt like after his First Vision. He knew it was true. He knew it! And he couldn't deny it, but he was despised for it, for bearing his soul and the truth. I bore my testimony to people who then spit in my face, who patronized me and the things I know to be true. There were different people, some said, "I have the Bible & you can't add to it"; others that they need more evidence to prove it to them. And another who said I'm in a cult. All three of these people spit in my face when I bore them my soul. I gave them the truth. It felt so awful because I realized this is my brother, this is my sister, they are rejecting all the happiness that God has to offer.

On March 5, 2006, the MTC screened a new hagiographic movie about Joseph Smith called *Joseph Smith: Prophet of the Restoration*. It was a movie we would later be able to use in our proselytizing efforts. I was moved to tears at the end—when Joseph Smith is murdered in a hail of bullets by a mob—in an overwhelming experience, and so was every elder in my dormitory room. We solemnly went back to our dorm rooms that night and held an impromptu testimony meeting before lights out. Everyone spoke of how we had all received such strong testimonies from the Holy Ghost that Joseph Smith was truly a prophet of God. I wrote to myself that night:

I know now more than ever that Joseph Smith was and is a prophet of the Most High God. He was a simple man, magnified by the Lord. I have received a strong witness & I pray that it doesn't fade. For any future struggle, DROP YOUR PRIDE! Stop any doubt before it ever gets into your head, Jeremy. You know that this is true in the moment you are writing it! Remember the feeling you had when you wrote this, and go out and share it with the world. God lives, He is your Father, Jesus is the Christ, He is your Savior, don't forget it. Joseph Smith was a prophet, remember the witness you had as you watched the film depicting his life. The Book of Mormon is true. The temple is truly of God, although you don't understand all, you know it is true, beautiful, amazing, and sacred. Gordon B. Hinckley is a living prophet.

The number of times I wrote something like this is actually rather amazing. During my time in the MTC, I wrote that "Joseph Smith was a Prophet" and "the Book of Mormon is the word of God, it is just what it claims to be" countless times.

Another event that deeply impacted me happened February 26, 2006. As I wrote in my journal that night, "When I arrived at the Lorenzo Snow Bldg. for the MTC Fireside ... to my absolute joy I saw the name Truman G. Madsen.... This was truly a tender mercy from the Lord. I can't explain the Spirit that was felt. Then afterwards I was privileged to meet him face to face and shake his hand [and] express some gratitude to him" because of how his lecturers had helped me gain a testimony of the Prophet Joseph Smith. "He grabbed my hand and put his arm around my neck and hugged me. I can't describe what it meant to me. This man's [lectures] solidified and led me for the first time to know that Joseph Smith was a Prophet. I thank God for that man and the opportunity."

Just before my time at the MTC ended, we went to the temple in Provo, Utah, to do the Endowment ceremony for the dead. As we walked into the Celestial Room, I had a spiritual impression. Filled with confidence that when these kinds of thoughts entered my head and felt just right, I could speak as definitively as Joseph Smith or any other prophet, I strolled up to my good friend Elder

T. J. McMullin, and I told him, "We are going to be companions at some point in Argentina, Elder." We embraced. Then I walked off.

MORMON MISSIONARY WORK in South America has deep ties to Buenos Aires. Although Argentina was not the first place Mormon missionaries visited in South America (missionaries had been sent to Chile, for instance, much earlier, but without notable success), Argentina was an important center for Mormonism, and Mormonism in Argentina began in the capital city of Buenos Aires. On Christmas Day, 1925, Mormon Apostle Melvin J. Ballard and other church leaders from North America gathered in Parque Tres de Febrero in Buenos Aires and offered a prayer, dediciating all of South America to the preaching of the Gospel. In a famous testimony meeting among German Mormon converts on July 4, 1926, Elder Ballard prophesied that the work would "grow slowly for a time here just as an oak grows slowly from an acorn".[7]

That prophecy was famous among the Mormons of Buenos Aires and was the motto of our mission, the Great Buenos Aires North Mission: "De Bellota al Roble" (from an acorn to an oak tree). It was a mentality that shaped the minds of the missionaries, helping them realize that sometimes the work would be slow and baptisms would be infrequent, but we would grow God's kingdom patiently, and we would find that we ourselves had grown in the same way, until all of us were oak trees in the faith.

Our group of seven missionaries from the MTC left for Buenos Aires on April 12, 2006. I had never traveled

---

[7] Matthew J. Grow, "The Modern Mormon Church", in *The Oxford Handbook of Mormonism*, ed. Terryl L. Givens and Philip L. Barlow (Oxford: Oxford University Press, 2015), 63.

via air—I had only flown in a small bush plane once as a child at an air show for a twenty-minute tour. A commercial airliner from Salt Lake to Dallas, then Dallas to Buenos Aires, was a life-changing experience, at once exhilarating and terrifying. Unable to sleep during the overnight flight, I arrived in Buenos Aires the next day exhausted. It was morning, and there was a dense blanket of fog spread over the city, with only the occasional building top poking through. We touched down at Ezeiza International just southwest of Buenos Aires. We met up with our contact at the airport and drove the short distance to the Argentina MTC, which is on the grounds of the Buenos Aires temple. There, we picked up the Latin American missionaries—four of them—and we met our mission president and his wife there on the temple grounds, where he reminded us that *this place* (the temple) was our goal, to get families baptized, converted, and sealed as families forever in the temple.

From there we all traveled to the mission president's posh suburban home in San Isidro, a wealthy neighborhood outside the capital city to the northwest. There at the mission home, I met my trainer, Elder Osvaldo Franco, a twenty-year-old missionary who was native to Argentina. He spoke only a few words of English, and to make things more difficult, he was from Córdoba and spoke with the famous accent from that region, with its sing-song quality and tendency to emphasize multiple syllables and draw them out.

I had been assigned, by revelation to the mission president, of course, to work with Elder Franco in a small branch of the church called Villa Adelina, which served parts of the urban sprawl to the north of Buenos Aires, including Boulogne, José León Suárez, Villa Adelina, and Carapachay, localities distinguishable only by dint of the street names and numbers instantaneously changing as you crossed the street from one municipal jurisdiction to the next—from 2341 Avellaneda on one side of the street to 645 Avenida San Martin on the other, for example.

We dropped off my belongings at our one-bedroom apartment in Boulogne, at 2540 Darragueira between Asamblea and Olazabal, only a few feet from an excellent pizzeria called El Duende. We did some grocery shopping because it was our weekly preparation day—a day missionaries received a partial reprieve from proselytizing to do laundry, shop for food, and perhaps see a sight or two. Then we headed out to the church building where, Elder Franco informed me, we hosted a weekly soccer event for teenagers and young adults to come and play on the only free grass soccer field around. We also taught an English class, which I learned that evening I would be in charge of. Elder Franco told me that several of our "investigators"— those who were regularly receiving lessons about the church—would be there. He assured me this was an extremely effective way to find people the Lord had prepared. I was skeptical and suspected Elder Franco liked to play soccer while making his English-speaking companion teach some people English phrases in the classroom inside in the meantime. Moreover, rule number one for being a missionary was that we were never to leave the presence of our companion. I was completely committed to being exactly obedient. He saw things more pragmatically. And such differences served as a more-than-mild source of tension during our months together.

Our walk over to the church that night was my introduction to street contacting—stopping random people to ask them if we could visit them in their home to share our message. You might think that doing this in another language is terrifying. But in reality, the language serves as a sort of shield. It emboldens you. I said things to people in

Spanish as a missionary that I certainly would have lacked the courage to say in English to a native English speaker. A high-ranking church leader who oversaw all the missions of Chile, Argentina, Paraguay, and Uruguay, Elder Lynn G. Robbins, had made a promise to our mission shortly before I arrived: if every missionary would simply do ten contacts a day, every day, without fail, the Lord would double baptisms in our mission. My mission president bore his testimony to us that this was true and a divine promise any number of times. And I felt the Holy Ghost tell me it was true too, so I was bound and determined. In my little white planner notebook that I kept in my pocket, I tallied every contact I ever made on my mission. I threw those notebooks away some years ago, or else I could tell you exactly how many people I approached during my mission. But it was close to ten per day, every day, so somewhere in the neighborhood of 6,600 people. Our mission was, for a long time, completely wrapped up in this promise from Elder Robbins. Buenos Aires, as a traditionally Catholic and European-influenced area, was not a hot spot for conversions, unlike other Latin American countries where baptisms flourished. Volume III of my mission journal has a motivational poem glued to the inside cover, underneath which I had written, "¿139 o 140?": Will you be the type of missionary companionship who does *139* contacts a week or one who does *140* (10 per day, 7 days a week, times 2)? We stopped individuals on the street, stood up in the front of packed buses and train cars, and spoke to basically every taxi driver we ever rode with. And that night, walking up to the church, I stopped a woman and began awkwardly to share the message of the Restored Gospel of Jesus Christ with her. "Hola, somos misioneros de la Iglesia de Jesucristo de los Santos de los Últimos Dìas. Tenemos un mensaje que nos gustaría ..." In her thick

Porteño accent she cut me off: "Discúlpame chico, que soy Católica." "Sorry, kid, I'm Catholic." And so it began, two years of giving every ounce of strength, of giving each waking moment, to Jesus Christ's restored church.

Mormon missionary work is, day to day, incredibly routine yet incredibly unpredictable at the same time. The routine was set by the missionary handbook:

- 6:30 A.M.—Arise, pray, exercise, and prepare for the day
- 7:30 A.M.—Breakfast
- 8:00 A.M.—Personal Scripture study
- 9:00 A.M.—Companionship study
- 9:30 A.M.—Language study
- 10:00 A.M.—Leave the house to proselytize
- Noon—Lunch
- 1:00 P.M.—Proselytize
- 9:00 P.M.—Return to the house, plan next day, write in journal
- 10:30 P.M.—Sleep

We had Christmas Day off, and we got to call home on Christmas and Mother's Day. But other than that, the same rigorous daily schedule followed day in and day out, rain or shine, hot or cold. Each day was centered around a few fixed appointments we had made through previous street contacting or perhaps referrals from church members or other people we were already teaching, with the rest of the time devoted to street contacting, visiting less-active members, trying to get referrals from members, and doing service projects. We rarely ate dinner, as that was seen as prime time for teaching, when the man of the house would be home from work. Mission rules prohibited us from teaching women without an adult man in the house, and the hope of all missionaries was, in any event, to baptize entire families, rather than individual members of a family. Our goal was to convert the father, because everyone else would likely follow if he joined.

The unpredictability of missionary life came from two sources: first, simply being in the street engaging with strangers for ten hours a day for two years will result in an enormous amount of strange happenings; second, as missionaries, we strove to be guided by the Holy Ghost, so our plans could turn on a dime if one of us felt the Spirit prompting us to do something else, to turn this corner, to go down that street, to turn around and go back and talk to someone we passed—all of which happened every day. We constantly prayed in alleyways for guidance from God on where to go to find those searching for the truth, and each subsequent thought, each impression, was at least potentially the Holy Ghost directing us where to go and what to do if we would simply have the courage to listen and obey. One time a companion and I, on a particularly trying day, ducked into an alley to pray, and the wind blew my planner open to the name of a member in the area. We decided to go there, and he was home! Our visit was spiritual and uplifting. For us, it was a miracle, even if a small one, and a clear manifestation of God's controlling hand in the smallest details of our work.

In total, I was assigned to serve in six different areas in our mission. Many of these places were functionally lower middle class to upper middle class, some even wealthy. But in almost all of them, as throughout the greater Buenos Aires metropolitan area, are countless slums, called *villas de emergencia*, or just *villas* for short (pronounced "*veesha*" with the Argentine accent). I will never forget my first entrance into a villa. On the southeast side of the city of Boulogne-Sur-Mer, there was an area stretching about seven blocks from Loria to Perito Moreno, bordered on the southwest by Guayaquil and on the northeast by the railroad tracks. The homes on the periphery of the neighborhood are typical lower-middle-class housing for Argentina. But as I passed a large dumpster fire, car tires and other trash ablaze sending a pitch-black column up into the humid Buenos Aires air, I could hardly believe my eyes. The muddy roads had foot-deep ruts, filled with stale water leaking over from gray-water ditches that lined just about every street in the city. There was garbage everywhere. Shacks made of cheap brick, corrugated metal, scrap wood, road signs, blue tarps, anything and everything, with large families packed inside, were built next to and even on top of each other, sometimes three stories high, jagged pieces of rebar sticking out every which way. The neighborhoods looked like impoverished Dr. Seuss architecture. When it rained, the sewers would overflow. I still remember seeing a huge pipe with who knows how many thousands of gallons of sewage just overflowing for hours on end up and into the streets. The mud would be up to our ankles. The overwhelming pungent odor of raw methane, like I had never encountered before, invaded my sinuses and lungs. I really couldn't believe the poverty.

But still, many people were happy, despite their circumstances. The first home of a Mormon family I ever entered in that villa was kept as clean as it could be, and the family just did their best to make their oversized shack a fortress against the evils that couldn't otherwise be kept from their family. I wrote that night, April 14, 2006, "We taught a family home evening [lesson,] Alarcón was the name of the [family]. It just hit me so hard, they lived in a villa and they seriously didn't have anything.... But they were so happy.... It was so great, but it was so humbling to think that sometimes we complain, we actually have the audacity to do that, where there are people who live in a shack and barely have anything."

The lives of people in these communities were hard. Drugs, drunkards, and severe mental health problems were ubiquitous. I recall seeing a poor man at the train station, not far from the entrance to the villa in Boulogne, in rags and with clear mental health and drug problems, laughing to himself and shaking, staring straight ahead at nothing in particular. There was an enormous, foaming, blackish-red pool of urine gushing from the bottom of his pantleg and running down to the edge of the platform. In Benavidez, where we lived only a few blocks from the poor sector of the town, I was washing dishes one day when a young man stopped outside our window, looked back and forth, pulled out a container of Poxi-Ran (an industrial epoxy glue), dipped a plastic bag into it, flipped the bag inside out, and then stuck his face in like a horse on a feed bag and huffed until he nearly lost consciousness. Another time in that same town, we came across a man outside of a small Catholic church in the town square, and he was beside himself, saying he needed money to buy a bus ticket to get his medication. I told him we didn't have any money (nor were we permitted to give our money away as missionaries), and all of a sudden, he screamed that this was it; he was done with it all! He darted toward the main drag and I yelled to my companion, "He's gonna kill himself!" We chased after him but were too far behind to stop him from diving headlong in front of a car. By God's grace, the car slammed on its brakes, colliding with the man's shoulder, and he bounced off the fender and rolled into the middle of the street, where traffic had come to an abrupt halt. He stood up, dazed but alive, and darted down another street. Another time, my companion and

I came across a man lying in the middle of the sidewalk as people casually walked past him. We approached, and I stooped down to see if he was all right. He reeked of alcohol, and I jumped back when he rolled toward me and a nickel-sized circular wound gushed blood from the middle of his forehead. At first, I thought someone had shot him but quickly realized he had passed out drunk next to a vacant lot that had a three-foot-tall piece of rebar sticking up out of the ground. He had come down straight on it and nearly impaled his face. Yet no one did a thing. People just walked by in an all-too-real-life demonstration of the Parable of the Good Samaritan. My companion and I screamed for someone to call an ambulance (we had no phone), and I tried to keep the man conscious until people finally intervened, and help arrived.

Violence, too, was a fairly common spectacle. A companion and I walked through one of the many Roma neighborhoods in the area where we were working and just escaped the crossfire of a shooting that sent a bullet straight out of the storefront window we had passed in front of only thirty to forty-five seconds earlier, during which we could hear a loud argument going on inside. We turned back and saw a man holding his bleeding abdomen jump into a car that screeched away as people were screaming for the police. But most of the violence or near violence I saw was directed at me or other missionaries. More than once I had men in my face, sometimes drunk, sometimes scarily sober, threatening to beat me up. You don't easily forget someone screaming nose to nose that he is going to split your head in two. I had a gun pulled on me twice. The first time it was pointed at my head, and I was so close I could see down the barrel. The other time was while I was serving as an assistant to the mission president. I went out with one of the zone leaders to visit his area in the neighborhood called Villa Lugano, home to the infamous "Ciudad Oculta", the Hidden City, an enormous slum in the southwest corner of Buenos Aires. We passed by the slum's most impressive landmark at the time (which has since been razed)—which sat on Piedra Buena Avenue between Ignacio de la Rosa and Hubac—a twelve-or-so-story abandoned hospital. We turned the corner onto Eva Perón Avenue to head toward the church to meet back up with the mission president, but we had only gone a few blocks when twenty yards ahead of us, I saw a young man, about our age, leaning against a wall, looking back and forth nervously, his right hand wrapped up in a T-shirt. I instantly knew we were about to get robbed, and sure enough, as we got near him, he stepped in front of us, grabbed me by the shirt collar, and shoved his T-shirt-covered hand (which held a small gun) forcefully into my stomach as he pulled my face close to his and demanded that I give him my cell phone. I told him I didn't have one. He then demanded money, so I gave him all I had: a five-peso bill. Elder Castillo similarly forked over what he had, secretly palming enough coins for the bus ride home. The young man turned down one of the countless alley-ways and headed into the heart of the Ciudad Occulta, shouting back at us, "Forgive me! God forgive me!"

Another time I had swapped companions for the day, and a fellow named Elder Peter Neilsen was with me. In the morning, we contacted a man named Joshua on the street, and he told us to come by his house that afternoon. Later that day, we approached the address we had been given, clapped outside the gate (you don't knock in Argentina—you clap), and asked for Joshua. A young boy said he would go get him, but all of a sudden, an enraged man burst from around the corner (not Joshua), cursing and screaming at us to leave. His eyes darted back and forth over the mess stacked up on either side of the small alleyway leading back to the house until they landed on a machete, which he ripped out of the mess, brandished directly at us with every permutation of Argentinian curse words I knew of, and ran at us ready to attack. We ran.

Frankly, my experiences were tame. I got spit on, but never hurt. Two missionaries in my district, serving in the rough neighborhoods of José León Suárez, showed up at district meeting one day, and the senior companion, Elder Juggler, had a sizeable goose egg on the side of his head from having been pistol-whipped the night before. Shortly after I left the mission, my mission president told me about two elders who had been violently attacked and beaten and showed up at the mission home dripping with blood from head to toe. This was, however, all to be expected. Being a missionary felt like living the Book of Acts. And I had covenanted in the temple, after all, before God, angels, and witnesses, that I would sacrifice *everything*, even my own life if necessary, to build up God's kingdom on Earth. I was never afraid of dying. I had no doubt whatsoever that angels stood by me continually and that I was doing God's work. As I wrote one October evening in 2006, "I am willing to give every last thing, all my heart, to be with [Christ]."

That willingness stemmed from my testimony, which was the primary thing I was working to pass on to others as a missionary. Indeed, it was the primary thing I was taught: to teach the message of Joseph Smith and the Restoration of the Gospel, get people to read the *Book of Mormon*, and get them to pray and ask God if it is true and then to *recognize* the answer when it came. And because we were looking for those whom God had already prepared to receive this message, we did not generally spend more than a few weeks attempting to teach someone. In one of our early large training meetings, called zone conferences, on

June 2, 2006, the main workshop taught by the mission president was entitled "How to Recognize the Voice of the Holy Ghost". Like anything else, being guided by God's quiet promptings was a *skill* that could be developed and nurtured through humble obedience to God. Among my notes are concepts such as "thoughts, feelings, comfort, serenity, impressions are more powerful and enduring" than things we see with our eyes. "God speaks to us through peace and tranquility." "Think of some time you have felt these feelings before, what did you do? Upon acting on those feelings, impressions, you will feel peace. Study it in your mind, then ask and you will feel." With each lesson we taught investigators, there were corresponding "commitments" that we asked people to keep: to read a passage from the *Book of Mormon*, to pray about Joseph Smith's prophetic calling, to attend church, and so on. If people failed to keep their commitments more than a few times, we moved on to find someone who was prepared. And our mission began aggressively by setting a baptismal commitment with people on the first lesson, which we would phrase: "If you were to come to know that Joseph Smith was a prophet and this message was true, would you commit to being baptized on X date?" (Usually it was a month from the current date, enough for them to attend church three weeks in a row, which was all that was required.) My missionary journals are replete with tales of this pattern, over and again. At my first baptism in April 2006, "the Spirit was so strong for all those present", and an investigator named Monica, who was unsure about getting baptized but who had come to see what it was like, met with us afterward. "We prayed afterward ... that she would receive an answer and she did, she is going to be baptized the 6th of May." She bore her testimony on May 7 during church and "told how when she prayed to know if she should get baptized, she heard a voice that sounded like her grandfather say, 'Moni,' and she got scared, but the next day we prayed together and received an answer and decided to be baptized."

That summer, after a particularly good lesson with a family, I wrote, "Tonight I was very blessed in a lesson about the Plan of Salvation, to be guided by the Spirit. I felt it so strongly, and so did they, although I felt not to put a specific date for baptism, we challenged them to be baptized and to repent. It was awesome." The next day, I wrote, "I just feel so good right [now], I have the Spirit with me and things are so good." My mission president accompanied us to teach that wonderful family who had been receiving the lessons for some time but just couldn't make the jump, and he took charge of the lesson. As I recorded it, "we had a very spiritual experience" and we had "received the impression", along with the mission president, "that it [was] [the wife's] time" to be baptized. I had "never felt so guided by the Spirit before. It felt like it was really speaking for me." And the mission president "bore his testimony so strongly, the Spirit was there and touched all of our hearts". But a few days later, the family, to my shock, told me they couldn't continue listening any longer. So, I wrote, we had "to stop visiting" them and find people who were prepared.

There was a particular turning point in my own spiritual development in September 2006. I had been transferred from the greater Buenos Aires area to the southern tip of the Patagonia in Rio Gallegos. Our mission had the domestic airport that connected to that city, and so it was part of our mission despite being 2,500 kilometers away and separated by numerous other missions.

My mission president and other mission leaders began urging us to hone the skill of receiving revelation, both to better our own lives and to help others convert to the Lord's church. The theme of the day-long workshop, for which we had fasted in preparation, was "how to be more guided by the Spirit". He based his workshop and sermon on *Doctrine and Covenants* 43, which teaches:

> And now, behold, I give unto you a commandment, that when ye are assembled together ye shall instruct and edify each other, that ye may know how to act and direct my church, how to act upon the points of my law and commandments, which I have given.
>
> And thus ye shall become instructed in the law of my church, and be sanctified by that which ye have received, and ye shall bind yourselves to act in all holiness before me—
>
> That inasmuch as ye do this, glory shall be added to the kingdom which ye have received. Inasmuch as ye do it not, it shall be taken, even that which ye have received.[8]

The point, he taught, was that we had to obligate ourselves to *act* upon spiritual impressions we received. He told us that each of us should commit to the following mantra: "Throughout the remainder of my life, I will seek to learn by what I hear, see, and feel. I will write down the important things I learn, and I will do them."[9] This was a quote from Mormon apostle Richard G. Scott, in which he taught how to receive revelation from God: we should place special emphasis on the feelings we have and the thoughts that come into our minds when we feel joy, peace, and serenity. By writing them down and *doing* those

---

[8] *Doctrine and Covenants* 43:8–10.

[9] Richard G. Scott, "How to Learn by the Spirit" (Brigham Young University Education Week devotional, August 21, 2007), https://www.churchof jesuschrist.org/study/new-era/2014/09/how-to-learn-by-the-spirit?lang=eng.

things, we would become ever more skilled in receiving revelation and knowing how to do God's will. We were always to carry a small notebook with us where we could jot these things down as they came to us throughout the day. But if we failed to act, "it shall be taken, even that which ye have received"[10]—that is, the Lord would not speak to us. This was all, of course, based on ideas rooted in the teachings of Joseph Smith. As he once explained, "a person may profit by noticing the first intimation of the spirit of revelation; for instance, when you feel pure intelligence flowing into you, it may give you sudden strokes of ideas, so that by noticing it, you may find it fulfilled the same day or soon ... those things that were presented unto your minds by the Spirit of God, will come to pass; and thus by learning the Spirit of God and understanding it, you may grow into the principle of revelation, until you become perfect in Christ Jesus."[11]

My journals throughout my mission are filled with hundreds, if not thousands, of bracketed thoughts or commitments—the brackets indicating spiritual impressions—ranging from the mundane—"[Use the telephone more in following up with investigators]"—to serious commitments for my future life—"[I must respect my wife more than my own life]"; "[I must marry in the temple with a worthy and righteous woman]"; "[Always pay your tithing]"; "[Always have family prayer]"—to affirmations of my testimony "[Jeremy, you know that (Gordon B. Hinckley) is a prophet.]" And with this increasing practice, I felt ever more confident that those thoughts and impressions came from God and were leading me along the path he wanted me to be on.

[10] *Doctrine and Covenants* 43:10.

[11] Joseph Smith, *History of the Church of Jesus Christ of Latter-day Saints* (Salt Lake City: Deseret Book, 1978), 3:381.

My journal reflects numerous instances when I recorded that I "felt something" or "felt impressed" or "just knew" what someone else needed to hear, and then the "Lord filled my mouth with the right words." I once testified to a tourist couple from Holland that I came across in Rio Gallegos, because I had been "impressed to tell [them] ... God has brought you all the way from Holland, across the ocean, to the tip of the American Continent in Rio Gallegos to this hotel in this very moment when we walked through this door so that you could hear this message, and that is the only reason God allowed you to come on this trip; it was so you could meet us." I then wrote, "It was a special experience." Nearly every entry discussing every lesson I taught contains some indication that I felt the Spirit and that I testified to the truthfulness of Joseph Smith and the Church of Jesus Christ of Latter-day Saints. Almost without fail, I "felt the Spirit so strongly when I testified ... about the Restoration of the Gospel of Jesus Christ."

I worked as hard as I possibly could during those two years and tried to be completely obedient to my mission presidents (I had two during my time there). I rose through the ranks, serving in mission leadership positions—district leader, trainer, zone leader. Ultimately, on November 17, 2007, my mission president called me to the mission home, asked me several moral worthiness questions, asked if I was willing to serve in whatever capacity I was asked to, and then "told me that the Lord had confirmed that now I need to be in the [mission] offices as his assistant." He assured "me several times that my assignment came from the Lord". I knew he was right, in part because my new companion was T.J. McMullin, whom I had approached in the Provo temple nearly two years before and, acting on a spiritual impression, boldly informed we would one day be companions. God fulfilled those impressions he sent, confirming to me that I understood how to recognize God's revelations to me personally. As assistant to the president, I helped run the entire mission, trained other missionaries and mission leaders, and spent many hours with the president in the process.

And what of Catholicism? Of course I encountered it in a place like Argentina, which, as secularized as it had become at that time, was still overwhelmingly culturally Catholic at the time. But my contacts were small and insignificant. I have to confess that in my earliest months in Argentina, I had a strong prejudice against the Catholic Church, largely from the apostasy narratives of Mormon leaders like Bruce R. McConkie and James E. Talmage: the Catholic Church was outright *evil*. I visited the Metropolitan Cathedral of Buenos Aires and the Church and Convent of Saint Francis and gawked at what I thought was the ostentatiousness of the place, particularly the main altar at the Metropolitan Cathedral, which my companion assured me with ghoulish hyperbole was made of solid silver. I even whispered to my companion inside the Church of Saint Francis that I "felt the Holy Ghost leave as soon as we walked in". I was also offended by the countless statuary throughout every city I ever went to—roadside shrines to licit saints like Our Lady of Luján and San Cayetano, as well as the extremely popular, but illicit, folk saint Gauchito Gil, were everywhere. I unequivocally saw this as blatant idolatry, condemned by the Bible. While my theological disagreement never diminished during my mission, my feelings about the Catholic Church changed rapidly while I was in Argentina. I came to see Catholics as largely good but benighted and superstitious people, the fruits of the Great Apostasy. But they had some truth, and the Catholic Church was likely to be a strong ally in the growing fight against militant secularism and atheism that was trending in the mid-2000s. I don't believe I ever really had a sustained conversation with a devout Catholic in those two years (nor did I ever hear about a particular famous archbishop, Jorge Bergoglio, who frequented the villas of Buenos Aires ministering to the poor and who would later become Pope Francis). The most consistent experience I had regarding Catholicism was being cut off mid-sentence and informed that someone was born Catholic and would die Catholic and had no interest.

When my two years in Argentina were finished, the two most formative years of my life up to that point, I had baptized or helped get baptized around twenty to twenty-five people, but whether or not they were converted and felt what I felt, there was no question that the most significant convert of my mission was me. On February 13, 2008, I wrote:

Well ... today is my last day in Argentina. There are many feelings in me. Mostly satisfaction. I feel grateful, and I feel that I have accomplished that which the Lord sent me here to do. As I prayed last [night] that feeling came to me, and the Lord calmed my soul a lot, the words of my patriarchal blessing came to my mind that I must remember the talents I've been given, and to use them to build God's kingdom, and ... that He will keep helping me progress. Last night I spent quite a while speaking with [the mission president and his wife] about schooling, dating/marriage, church activity, work. We also talked about pitfalls [to avoid when coming home from my mission]. He said that two pitfalls to really stay clear of are 1) thinking you are invincible against temptation and [2)] ... thinking that you have to "relax" and "come back to the real world." I must keep planning and living in the same way.

4

Building Up Heavenly Father's Kingdom

"INSTITUTE" IS THE NAME for regular religious studies courses for young adults in the Mormon Church. I walked into the institute building on February 19, 2008, just days after returning from my mission. I knew everybody there from my small town except one person: a cute redhead with her curly hair pulled back, wearing a BYU sweater. She opened the institute meeting before the instructor taught, and I could tell she was an active member of the church. After religious instruction, we all headed over to the church building where, inside the gym, they had set up a pinewood derby track. It was clean fun, classically Mormon in every way.

I took a moment to speak to the redhead. Her name was Carly Torgerson. She had graduated from BYU with an English degree and had taken a job in middle-of-nowhere Blanding to teach at the high school. She had served a mission to Honduras and spoke Spanish. I was interested immediately.

Every aspect of my life was subject to intense prayer and thought, looking for God's guidance during a time that my mission leaders had taught me was the most crucial decade of my life—a time when I would make decisions that would have ramifications not just for decades to follow, but really, for eternity. It is not surprising to see my journals full of internal dialogue, prayer, and bracketed impressions, as I sorted out what I should do with my life, what I should study, what career I should pursue, and whom I should date and marry.

I loved the Scriptures as a missionary and had a desire perhaps to study ancient languages and the Bible. I pondered for a while whether to study Hebrew and Arabic, but, on February 23, 2008, I recorded that I "had [a] strange impression" that I was "trying to confirm" about "not studying Hebrew ... I want to, but something is telling me no." So I abandoned the idea altogether. A month later, I recorded, "I feel impressed to write that if I involve Spanish into my education, it will be a blessing to me, my family, and many other people." And just a little more than two weeks later, on April 6, 2008, definitively and in brackets so as to remind myself that I understood this as an impression from the Holy Ghost: "[I am to be a lawyer.]"

At the same time, I was pursuing Carly. At first, on a thinly veiled pretense, I mustered the courage to ask her for some book recommendations. She made a couple of recommendations and lent me her copies, but I didn't make it more than a few pages in. A short while later, on March 12, 2008, I decided to ask her on a date. "She said yes", I wrote excitedly. We needed to set the details, so I went to her classroom the next day. I was working as a school-bus mechanic at the time, so I trudged into her classroom wearing a mechanic's shirt smeared with grease, steel-toed boots, Dickies jeans, and a ball cap and told her we would go to the Valley of the Gods, a scenic area near Monument Valley, Utah. I had my mom help me put together a picnic lunch of fried chicken, grapes, and some potato salad, and I put it in the cooler and picked Carly up one Saturday morning. We spent the whole day together. A couple weeks later, I wrote, "She seems like a good person. I am going to ask her out again." We continued to see each other, and I was falling in love and already thinking of marriage.

I am grateful to my mother and some other people in my life who gave me some of the most critical marriage advice I ever received in the Mormon context: dating and deciding to marry someone is *not* about seeking personal revelation to know who you are supposed to marry, as if there were some special someone out there and you were trying to figure it out and not pick the wrong person. There is no "one". Rather, I was supposed to find someone I wanted to marry, someone I loved, and someone I would *choose* to love, to make her happiness greater than my own. I was then to ask God if that decision was okay and trust that if it was not, he would let me know. My mission president had taught me similar things.

I say this because, as with all the decisions in my young adult life, I tried to make this decision the way the church taught me to. And that meant that marriage was a subject on which I needed to think carefully and pray and seek for answers, in the same way that we seek for answers on other topics. But the process was complicated. Everything was going great. Carly and I continued to date, and I fell right in love, despite how short our time together was. She was simply everything I could have ever wanted in a spouse. As I recorded after a particularly memorable date we had one night, "I love this girl. Every minute I'm with her, when I have to leave, I don't want to." But things were obviously moving fast. And she was much more cautious than I was. I started to talk about marriage, and her eyes popped. Her parents were also skeptical of our relationship at first. They worried that I was a young, freshly returned missionary, full of fire for the church, but that—as with many young Mormon men—maybe the fire wouldn't last. The worst decision either of us could make, from our own perspectives, was to wind up with someone whose commitment to the church was not on par with our own. From my perspective, I was fully committed, and so was she. She, too, had a firm testimony of the church, and she was committed to living the life that I wanted to live—one rooted in the church, raising a family, and keeping our covenants with God. But we had a bit of a choice coming up. I was going to be moving across the state to start college at Southern Utah University, in Cedar City, Utah. Carly was reaching the point at which she had to decide to renew her teaching contract with the high school in Blanding. I continued to press the issue; she took her time.

At one point, I had done so much thinking and praying, I finally told God I had really thought about this, and that I wanted to marry her. I asked him to let me know if there was a problem with that. I sat quietly in prayer, listening for that still small voice I had come to recognize. In my mind, everything seemed great—she was a good person, we shared the same commitment to the church, we both wanted to start a family immediately, and so on. As I knelt alone in my room, however, the thought "no" crossed my mind. I began to ruminate on it, and I felt utterly confused. This seemed, as Mormon doctrine teaches, like the opposite of the "burning in the bosom" that the Holy Ghost uses to tell us something is good and true and okay and felt instead, perhaps, like the "stupor of thought" that signaled a negative response from God. I was devastated. The thought came out of nowhere and was completely contrary to every other indication that was going on in my life. It was late, and I went to bed, but I could hardly sleep.

The next morning, my mind was racked with uncertainty. I prayed more, trying to make sure of my feelings.

I poured my heart out to God about how much I loved Carly and how much sense all of this made. But nothing. No response. No feelings. I sat down at my computer and turned on some music, the famous Mormon hymn "Come, Come Ye Saints", composed and sung by the Mormon pioneers as an anthem of hope in the dark time they spent crossing the plains of the United States. As the music started and I pondered my future with Carly, emotion swept over me, and an immense feeling of happiness, peace, and joy filled my heart. I knew it was okay for me to marry Carly. The choice was up to her, but I knew it was okay. I had received a revelation. Carly's came shortly thereafter, on June 1, 2008. She texted me before a church fireside meeting that evening and said, "Come over early, I want to tell you something." I wrote, "She was literally shaking with excitement. I've never seen her so happy. She had a revelation.... The relief and happiness I felt was so great. We are so happy. I learned something very great, [contained in] the line in my patriarchal blessing [which] says, ... 'You will be guided by the Spirit in the things you are to do.' My trust and faith have increased tenfold today."

I proposed a few days later, and we were married that fall, September 6, 2008, in the Los Angeles temple, where we were sealed together forever as husband and wife. If we were true and faithful to the covenants we had each made in the temple when we received our endowments and to the covenants we made when we were married in the temple sealing ceremony, one day, we would both receive the greatest blessings our Heavenly Father had to offer: exaltation in the Celestial Kingdom. We would become like God. I wrote that day, "The things I learned [in the temple today] by instruction and by the Spirit were so sacred. They cannot be written."

We set about living our life as we had always been taught to. Our commitment stemmed from our strong testimonies from the Holy Ghost. At the first General Conference of the tenure of new church president Thomas Monson, in April 2008, there was an opportunity to "sustain" his calling—a visual vote of sorts where church members in attendance (and at home watching on TV) raise their hands in a show of support for the new church leader, as a sign they promise to sustain him and follow him. That day I recorded, "I received a sure witness by the Spirit that Thomas S. Monson is the Lord's anointed prophet, seer, and revelator. I felt that undeniably. I pledge to do everything he asks of me. And to encourage others to do the same." That sentiment epitomizes how Carly and I felt about our commitment to the church, and it showed in our actions.

Carly immediately became pregnant after our marriage—and I mean immediately. I started attending college to pursue my degree at Southern Utah University, so I could then prepare to go to law school. And we modeled our new family's spiritual life on the lives we had been given by our parents: daily prayer together, weekly family home evening on Mondays, regular attendance together at the temple, attendance each Sunday at church. We were, by any measure, poor. I once recorded in my journal during that first year of marriage, "I went on a date with Carly today. We spent 3 dollars on a burger and two ice cream cones." But we paid our tithing faithfully and never faltered. And of course, we served in whatever callings were extended to us at the time, giving our best efforts to fulfill what we generally took as being callings from God to serve in our ward.

One particularly memorable example of my commitment to the church took place on the night of February 28, 2009, and into the morning of March 1. That weekend was Stake Conference, a semiannual two-day conference for which regular Sunday meetings are canceled and an entire Mormon stake (made up of a half dozen or more congregations) meets together to be taught by the stake president and other stake leaders. Frequently, these meetings will include special visits by the church's "general authorities", members of the Quorums of Seventy or, sometimes even the Quorum of the Twelve Apostles. At that conference, two lower-level general authorities, "Seventies" of varying ranks, were visiting: Elder Kenneth Packer and an Elder Wheeler. I was invited to an early-morning meeting for local ward leadership throughout our stake in which these men would be speaking and teaching us in a fairly intimate setting.

For about a week before, I had been having random sharp pains in my left side and near my bladder, usually only lasting a moment or two, and I wrote them off. But the night of February 28, as I got into bed, I began having an uncontrollable pain in my left side, worse than any other pain I had experienced before or have since. As I wrote the next day in my journal, "I was on the floor shaking uncontrollably, wincing, and wrenching from pain." My wife called some friends who came and gave me a priesthood blessing, scooped me off the floor, and got me to the hospital, where I ultimately passed a kidney stone. I did not leave the emergency room until two or three o'clock Sunday morning. But I went home, slept for a couple of hours, and then went to the leadership meeting, which began at 6:30 A.M., pale and exhausted. I found that I needed to go into the hallway for a sip of water and to take some pain medication. And I was so mortified that I had to get up and leave during the middle of Elder Wheeler's presentation that I found him afterward to apologize profusely. I was fully committed.

More serious leadership responsibilities, and thus more serious strains on what little time I felt I had between full-time school and my job, were soon in the cards. For years, beginning on my mission, various church members and leaders had expressed the belief, opinion, or sometimes even "impression" that I would one day serve in significant roles in the church. I had always been taught, like every Mormon of the time, that we do not seek out callings or relish getting them. We simply and humbly accept the calling wherever we are asked to serve, whether it is a high-profile position or serving in the nursery with the toddlers so their parents can go to Sunday School without interruption. But on April 19, 2009, "I received a phone call and was scheduled to have an interview . . . with President Johnson from the University 3rd Stake." On April 21, Carly and I went to his office, and "they [the entire stake presidency] extended a call to me to be the 2nd Counselor in the 8th Ward Bishopric"—a ward for young adult singles. I "felt really anxious" about it, but also felt "at peace knowing the Lord has called me". One of the counselors to the stake president said to me, "Have confidence. You have been called by prophecy and will be set apart by those in authority. And remember as you sit and teach people your own age and sign [that] their temple recommends what Paul said to Timothy: 'Let no man despise thy youth, but be an example of the believers.'" Later that year, I recorded, "I just had an interview with . . . the 2nd Counselor in the Stake Presidency. . . . He told me that my time here [in the bishopric] was only training and a proving ground . . . and that if I prepare, I will someday be called to heavy responsibility in the Kingdom."

Being in a bishopric at age twenty-two, dirt poor, my time stretched as far as it could be, was difficult. Fatherhood came on top of it all. On June 5, 2009, I wrote,

"At 12:11 pm Raymond John Christiansen came into the world. He is beautiful. He is so perfect. His delivery was an exhausting experience physically, mentally, emotionally, and spiritually. Our prayers and faith and patience were all put to the test. Carly's endurance was tried to her limits. How eternally grateful I am for her and for her sacrifices. I pray that I may be worthy to take her and Raymond back to the presence of the Father."

But the stresses of fatherhood proved significant for me. Although it is a common Mormon axiom that "No success can compensate for failure in the home", I, like many, did not see any necessary contradiction between being successful in my worldly endeavors and an active commitment to my family and the church. Indeed, many successful Mormon men in my life, men I looked up to, routinely spoke of the significant amounts of family time they sacrificed to serve the Lord in their callings and to be successful in their professions as well. Moreover, my patriarchal blessing had promised me that my "success in life will allow [me] to do the things our Father in Heaven has sent [me] here to do."

So I saw my educational pursuits as being inextricably interwoven with God's plan for me, and my success seemed to confirm that this was part of this plan. Entries like "I got an A on my chem lab!!!... I am grateful to the Lord for His help and grace which gave me the capacity to do well" and "Today I got my chemistry test back. 103%!! I was so happy and I felt so humbled. I am so grateful for the many blessings of the Lord" and "I got 100% on my accounting test. I am very happy about it. I am grateful to the Lord for His help and strength. I know He will continue to strengthen me" and "I did very well on both my Econ and Business Law exams. I am thankful for the help I receive from the Lord to do well"—these kinds of entries fill my journals during that time. Each test was a matter of faith as much as an intellectual exercise. Priesthood leaders around me were confirming this growing sense of the tie between my academic success and God's plan for my life in a very explicit way. On June 7, 2009, I recorded, "I received a blessing from Brother Heuett", the first counselor in the bishopric and a man of considerable church leadership experience. "It was powerful. The Lord promised me success on my test tomorrow, my classes, and my education entirely."

Around October 14 of that year, I, like many other people in the United States, fell severely ill with the H1N1 influenza virus or "swine flu". For whatever reason, I was hit especially hard, and on October 16, 2009, I collapsed at home alone with a temperature spiking well above 105 degrees. I managed to call 911 on the floor and was drifting in and out of consciousness, to the point that when the operator began to ask me if I had children and what their names and birthdays were, despite Raymond having been born only a few months earlier, I could not recall his name or birthday. My wife arrived just before the ambulance did. I was admitted to the hospital, and after being discharged, I spent a few weeks at home recovering.

I do not recall why exactly, but I purchased the famous Paul Schofield movie about the life of Saint Thomas More, *A Man for All Seasons*, to watch during my recovery. I was incredibly moved by his example and his faith and willingness to die, feeling the Spirit testify to me of the integrity of this man's life. He inspired me to want to be a person, and lawyer, of integrity. Yet I remember the distinct confusion at times of not knowing how to reconcile his death and the powerful feelings I had with the reality that he was, according to the Mormon Church, definitively on the wrong side of the Reformation. Indeed, More is well known as a fiery antagonist of the Reformers, having been personally commissioned by the English Church to read the works of and write polemical responses to Tyndale, Luther, and others. Around the time I bought the movie, in fact, the church had released a series of short videos celebrating the martyrs of the Reformation, including William Tyndale. And I had also been moved, and felt the Spirit, upon watching his story. I considered him to be a hero whose brave actions helped set the stage, ultimately, for the Restoration of the Gospel in America by making the Bible available in English. I did not give too much thought to the conflict, however, as the church taught that those in life who did not receive the Gospel but held fast to their conscience would be given the chance to receive the Restored Gospel in the spirit world and thus ultimately to receive the fullness of Christ's teachings. But Saint Thomas More would begin reappearing in my life at critical intervals from then on.

One perceived conflict I did give some thought to at that time was that between faith and reason. In the fall of 2009, I enrolled in a philosophy class that was an introduction to logic and logical reasoning. It covered the basics of formal logic, deductive and inductive reasoning, valid and invalid deductive arguments, and informal logical fallacies. I loved the class, but it made me uneasy, especially when it came to applying the same standards of reasoning I was learning in class to the church and its teachings. On September 18, 2009, I wrote, somewhat alarmed, "I have seen how ... people tr[y] to blow out our candle of faith. My reasoning and logic class is one of those. The books I read at times are critical of belief in God. I feel the adversary's tactics to use logic when evaluating some aspects of the Gospel. But I will not give in." At that time, I made a conscious decision not to apply those standards to my faith.

As with my other classes, I did well in this one too, and I wrote later that semester, "The Lord ... has helped me to truly think more logically. I recognize that it is a tool that is adequate for some uses, awesome for others, and totally useless in others still."

This was a conscious application of a framework of thinking I heard during an April 2008 General Conference address by Elder Dallin Oaks—one of the church's twelve apostles, and, prior to that, a successful legal academic and a Utah Supreme Court justice. The talk, called "Testimony", posited that the propositions that I "know the Gospel is true", that "I know it is cold outside", or that "I know I love my wife" are positing "three different kinds of knowledge, each learned in a different way." He noted, "Knowledge of outside temperature can be verified by scientific proof. Knowledge that we love our spouse is personal and subjective. While not capable of scientific proof, it is still important." He then taught that "one of the greatest things about our Heavenly Father's plan for his children is that each of us can know the truth of that plan for ourselves. That revealed knowledge does not come from books, from scientific proof, or from intellectual pondering." Rather, "we ... receive that knowledge directly from our Heavenly Father through the witness of the Holy Ghost." And "when we know spiritual truths by spiritual means, we can be just as sure of that knowledge as scholars and scientists are of the different kinds of knowledge they have acquired by different methods." He concluded, "Anyone can disagree with our personal testimony, but no one can refute it."[1] I took that message to heart throughout my undergraduate years.

[1] Dallin H. Oaks, "Testimony", Ensign, May 2008, https://www.churchof jesuschrist.org/study/ensign/2008/05/testimony?lang=eng.

Our life continued apace. My calling in the bishopric was a great experience for us, and I learned a great deal about service in the Mormon Church from the bishop with whom I worked. It was a busy time, but I felt the constant presence of God and his reassuring hand in my life. Each semester grades came out, and each semester I continued to get straight As. I was released from my calling in the bishopric after about a year, which was the normal time for younger men to serve in those positions in the singles wards. As I was released from that calling in a private meeting with the stake presidency, the stake president looked at me, crying, and said, "I testify to you that there is a reason you served here." I, too, felt that same conviction, writing in my journal later that day, "I know the Lord has much in store for me to do. I need to get ready." Around that time, as I recorded in my journal, "I had a dream. I was upset with someone because of their fault. I was stewing over it, when I looked up, and I saw the Savior walk towards me. The feeling was indescribable. His look was one that instantly communicated His love for me, and for him with whom I was upset. 'Show him mercy. Let it go' were [the words] in His eyes. I saw His hand; it was His right hand. I saw and touched the nail print in His palm and kissed it. I felt His love and encouragement. Then it was over." It was an intense experience, not the first sort of dream that had powerfully confirmed my testimony, but a notable one to be sure.

As we returned to our ward, I was called as Gospel doctrine teacher, a calling that I loved and that was much less demanding on my time. That was just as well because I was continuing to prepare for the LSAT and for law school, and our second child, Virginia, was born that fall, in November 2010. Two children are somehow many more than one. Eventually, I applied to law schools all across the country, and as acceptances and scholarship offers rolled in, I fretted over where to go, over where would be the best for our family, over where would be the place God wanted me to be. In March 20, 2011, I had a sit-down meeting with the associate general counsel for the church. One of my professors from school had introduced me to him. He had been a managing partner over several Eastern European offices of a major international law firm. I met him at his office in the church's headquarters in Salt Lake City. He advised me as I recorded it (likely in paraphrase), "Don't be afraid to work for a big law firm.... People make excuses and are lazy and don't manage their time well. Manage your time, be disciplined, work hard, and you will have time for family and callings." He specifically told me that many high-ranking leaders of the church had been lawyers and had sacrificed time with their families because of their busy professions and church service, but that the Lord blessed them for it. A time for a decision was approaching. We were praying for answers, and ultimately, we made the decision, and felt good about it, for me to attend law school at the University of Utah in Salt Lake City. "We made the choice, prayed, and received a confirmation. We are very excited. The Lord guided us and I am grateful for it," I wrote.

5

The Dark Night of the Soul, Part I

LAW SCHOOL IS, as the saying goes, a jealous mistress. It is an incredibly challenging time for anyone, intellectually and emotionally. A group of already-neurotic, status-obsessed, grade-obsessed overachievers are tossed into the fray with one another; given unreasonable amounts of daily reading; called on at random by professors who grill them about details of the cases assigned—always raising *more* questions and never giving any answers in a process in which it is hoped the students will simply discern the law from these Socratic dialogues; usually given a single, hours-long examination at the end of the semester that will determine their entire grade for the course; and, for good measure, graded on a forced curve, meaning only a couple of As are given out in each class. For the uninitiated, it is hard to emphasize how important grades are in law school and in the culture of the profession more generally. They are— for better or worse—a heuristic used to sort law students to determine who will be the ones to get on the school's academic law review journal and obtain future prospects for working for prestigious judges and at fancy law firms. I had such ambitions, and as important as grades and other outward markers of success were in general, they became even more so for someone like me: someone with ambition to move in the highest levels of the profession, but who was not at a name-brand school like Harvard or Yale. Don't get me wrong: my alma matter is a great institution, and its top students can compete with the top students from any law school in the nation—but that is the key. To move into the world of "big law" and prestigious federal clerkships, it was not sufficient to be in the top 5 percent of your class at my school; you had to be more one of the top five *students* to get a serious look when your competitors are top students from Harvard, Yale, Chicago, Columbia, and so on.

I threw myself into law school with excessive devotion, usually arriving each morning around six-thirty and staying late into the night. It is not surprising that my journal records, month after month, "I feel so buried.... Law school is incredibly stressful"; "I feel so in over my head right now"; "I am SO STRESSED! I really want to tear my hair out because I need like 6 or 7 more hours in a day"; "I feel like the weight of school is crushing me." On top of that, I was quickly given significant responsibility in a new calling in our ward. On October 16, 2011, "I was called to be the 2nd Counselor in the Elder's Quorum Presidency.... I feel so overwhelmed right now." The Elders Quorum presidency has a very significant amount of responsibility in a ward, running, what was then known as the "home teaching" program. Each family in the ward is assigned a companionship of two priesthood holders who go and visit their assigned families each month, check in on their needs and welfare, deliver a spiritual message of some kind, and report back. Making those assignments, encouraging men to go on their visits, following up, and reporting to ward and stake leadership on those efforts was time consuming. We had multiple weekly meetings, had to extend callings to others in the ward, ran a Sunday-school-style class each Sunday, and were frequently called on to help move members in and out of the ward and do extensive service projects, from re-staining a deck to mowing lawns to plowing the widows' driveways when it snowed on Sunday mornings.

But the conviction of having been called by God to do this helped me trust that I could do it all. One quiet morning in the law library, I found myself alone in the stacks and stumbled upon a section that contained old law reports printed in the 1700s. They smelled of must and rotting leather. They left a grimy feeling on your hands when you touched them. I was surprised the books were out in the stacks to begin with. But as I inspected them, I saw they were reported trials of England, going back centuries. I opened one of the early volumes in the series and looked through it, and there I found the reported trial of Sir Thomas More, which occurred in July 1535. I read it there alone in the still hours before class. Again, I could not help but be fascinated and moved by his integrity and by his devotion to his faith and to serving his country. I wrote in my journal, "I have been reflecting a lot on the life of Sir Thomas More. I want to be as true to my faith and my conscience as he was to his." He inspired me.

Through thought and prayer, I set a list of aggressive goals for myself, including finishing in the top 5 percent of my class. I really wanted to get a 4.0, which seemed very far-fetched, so that I could get clerkships with prestigious judges and go on to work in my dream profession—doing constitutional and appellate law in a large law firm. The goal became an unhealthy obsession (something I realized in retrospect). Time and again, as I pondered these goals and asked God to help me achieve them, I felt the Holy Ghost testify to me as I read the words of a revelation to Joseph Smith, recorded now in *Doctrine and Covenants*:

Verily I say unto you my friends, fear not, let your hearts be comforted; yea, rejoice evermore, and in everything give thanks; Waiting patiently on the Lord, for your prayers have entered into the ears of the Lord of Sabaoth, and are recorded with this seal and testament—the Lord hath sworn and decreed that they shall be granted. Therefore, he giveth this promise unto you, with an immutable covenant that they shall be fulfilled.[1]

Just as my first finals period started, the Elders Quorum president gave me a blessing. As I recorded it, "He blessed me that I would work hard and perform how I know I can and how Heavenly Father knows I can." I poured all my efforts into doing the very best that I could that first semester. For my contracts course alone, I took four four-hour-long practice exams in the space of just six days. I had a twenty-page outline in ten-point font that I had memorized verbatim, every word, by pacing back and forth alone in my house over Thanksgiving break while my family traveled so I could have time to study alone and get prepared for finals. I wrote, just before exams, "I felt as I prayed to my Heavenly Father that I am prepared enough." I did the same thing, exam after exam. My civil procedure exam was so difficult that I left the room after submitting my answers and immediately broke down, convinced I had surely failed. I went home and began Christmas break with my wife and kids and watched *It's a Wonderful Life* to try and cheer myself up. And then I waited.

On January 16, 2012, I wrote, "Grades came out last Friday. . . . I was downtown picking up a pro bono project. I called Carly when I left because I knew that grades had posted in the meantime. Our plan was for her to see them first. When she picked up the phone she said, 'Jeremy,

---

[1] *Doctrine and Covenants* 98.

I cried.' My heart sank. 'You got a 4.0.' I almost passed out. I started sobbing as I walked down Main Street to the train station. The Lord has blessed me...." It did not just feel like a worldly accomplishment. Rather, it felt like a deep spiritual sign of sorts to me, that my impressions were correct and that I was indeed on a path that God was preparing for me. The next semester, I again got a 4.0, tying with a good friend of mine for first in our class. Each semester, not only did I get As, but with only one exception, I got the highest A in each section, receiving numerous "book awards", as they are known in law school. I had little trouble securing a high-paying summer job at a prestigious law firm in Salt Lake City, and it seemed clear I would be in a competitive position to secure a postgraduate judicial clerkship, as long as I could keep things up. Our third child was born that summer. We named him Rex Lee Christiansen, after my legal hero, Rex E. Lee, who was a famous United States Supreme Court litigator, the founding dean of BYU's law school, a faithful Mormon, and by all accounts (Mormon and non-Mormon) an incredibly good human being. I was also selected to join the *Utah Law Review*, a prestigious position in which law students function as editors of the schools' academic journal, ultimately being elected to the *Law Review*'s executive board.

A common refrain in the legal world is that the reward for winning the pie-eating contest is more pie. I grew significantly in my capacity to handle the stress that law school, family life, and church life put on me that first year. But more came. As I wrote in September 2012, there were rumors that the Elders Quorum presidency I was in was going to be dissolved and that there were so many members in the ward that they were going to establish a second Elders Quorum to provide for everyone adequately.

I had some foreboding about that, writing, "I am nervous that I may be called into one of the new presidencies as president"—a calling with even *more* responsibly than I had at the time. But I was committed, noting, "I have ... already spoken with the Lord and told him that I will do whatever I'm asked to do." Things remained quiet, however, for a while longer.

In early November, the Elder's Quorum president called me "to tell me which side of the ward I should 'strongly consider choosing to focus my attention [on]'". He told me that my name and the name of one other counselor were the only ones under consideration for the two new president positions. I wrote in my journal, "I don't know why, but this whole thing has just not felt good. I know this, however: The Church is true, President McKeown [the stake president] will do the right thing because he is called of God. Whatever he asks me to do, I will do it." A few days later, I recorded, "I am one of the new elders quorum presidents."

When you receive a calling in the Mormon Church, you receive a special blessing from a priesthood leader called a "setting apart", in which you are given authority to carry out your calling, and usually an extemporaneous blessing is pronounced on you to guide you. I was set apart by the stake president on November 11, 2012. He knew me and what was going on in my life, but in a moment of what felt like God again speaking directly to me, he blessed me in a very unusual and specific way. Finals were just around the bend, and I was, as usual, feeling a lot of stress about the outcome. I will never forget what he said to me: "I promise you that as you prepare for your classes and exams, you will perform as you expect to on those exams." This was a massive comfort to me, and I felt a swirl of emotion in my heart, as I had before in so many instances in the church. I felt a deep assurance that if I just kept doing my part, I would keep up my 4.0. After all, I had achieved that unlikely outcome two semesters in a row, earning the highest marks in almost every section. Exams came and went. But I was still nervous. Disquieted by the uncertainty of it all, as I recorded in my journal on January 2, 2013,

> I picked up my scriptures hoping to just get guidance. As I touched them, D&C 98 came to mind. It's a section the Lord has used to assure me in law school on various occasions.... I simply opened the book up, and it was upside down. When I flipped it over, I had turned to D&C [*Doctrine and Covenants*] 98. "Verily I say unto you ... fear not, let your hearts be comforted; yea, rejoice evermore, and in everything give thanks: Waiting patiently on the Lord, for your prayers have entered into the ears of the Lord of Sabaoth, and are recorded with this seal and testament—the Lord hath sworn and declared that they shall be granted." As had happened so many other times before, when I felt like I needed God's reassurance and guidance so desperately, He again answered me, speaking through the scriptures, straight to me. Emotion overwhelmed me and I felt a strong feeling of calm, and the thoughts of the Stake President's blessing came to my mind: I had prepared as I had before, and was promised that I would perform as I expected.

I fully realize how ridiculous what I am about to write sounds. But it is true and served as a critical catalyst. The morning of January 6, 2013, I sat in my bedroom nervously waiting. I had pushed the refresh button several times, but no grades had come up yet. It was early in the morning, and I needed to prepare for church. "I'll just hit refresh one more time before I go get ready." And there it was. "B+ Constitutional Law II". I could not believe my eyes, and my heart sank. Such a grade may not seem like a big deal; indeed, it might even seem good. But in law school, things are not as they seem, and for someone in my position, a grade that was not at the top of the curve was a serious hit to my transcript and professional aspirations.

I tried to brush it off and just accept that I hadn't performed my best, for whatever reason. In the next few days, the rest of my grades poured in, "A", "A", "A" … But something was wrong, and it just kept getting worse. Over the ensuing weeks, my journal entries reflect a dark turn. I was full of self-loathing and questioning over how I could have failed to perform on this exam, how I could have so patently misunderstood my own desires for God's will. Months later, I was still agonizing over it all, referencing "D&C 98" and reassuring myself that God "*will* answer your prayers" and provide answers about the "B+".

Life pressures continued to mount. Not only was I serving as the Elders Quorum president, but my wife was then called to be in the Relief Society presidency (meaning she had a very similar role, but overseeing all the women in the ward). I began to feel bitter, at times even angry, over what had happened. "It has been a difficult 8 months for me. I have let myself stray from the Lord. I have blamed him for getting a bad grade last fall.… I don't know what would happen to me if I died today." On two significant occasions, "I imagined killing myself" and "dwelt on these thoughts for … maybe an hour" each time. On one of those occasions, the thought of nonexistence filled me with calm and wrapped me up like a warm blanket. And something somehow surfaced in my internal dialogue: "Jeremy, you have depression. This is not okay. You need help." In October 2013, I spoke with my wife, and we decided I should go see a doctor. Serious depression ran in my family, but this was my first encounter not just with being blue for a while, but with a months-long blackness that culminated in suicidal ideation. A wonderful doctor at the Madsen Clinic in Salt Lake City helped me make a lot of lifestyle changes that, over time, helped me recover from that terrible episode.

But something else began that morning: doubt. Sitting at my computer and staring at a cold, hard reality that contradicted what a priesthood leader, under inspiration, had actually promised to me, and what I had simultaneously felt was true in that same way I had felt so many other things, shook something loose. I had experienced priesthood leaders speaking "under inspiration" before when they clearly weren't. My faith was not so shallow as to fail to account for that. I knew that sometimes a priesthood leader is mistaken, and sometimes *we* are mistaken; discerning God's voice in our life is not an easy task. Yet something was different this time. Reality just did not care what my stake president had uttered in the name of the Lord that I had fully believed. I did not perform as I had expected to. Indeed, no one really expected that; one law professor at my school, upon finding out, even offered to intervene to try to get the grade challenged because it was so uncharacteristic. For months I battled depression and found it "difficult to be motivated", writing "All is numb." By the spring of 2014, I started to express a "need to spill my thoughts" and admit that "I just don't feel very good about where I am at in life right now", hoping I could "find my way through all the doubt and confusion I've been in for so long".

I graduated from law school on May 9, 2014, tied for third in my law school class, with two judicial clerkships lined up for 2014–2015 and 2015–2016 and an offer to return to the law firm in Salt Lake City I worked for each summer. In the broader scheme, things worked out, although angst plagued me. I did not receive an offer for a very prestigious employment opportunity for which I interviewed, and it was made clear to me in no uncertain terms that the B+ was the reason I was not getting the job—those things really do matter in the world of law, at least on the margins, when there is a highly competitive and prestigious position on the line.

The day I graduated, I wrote, "It's interesting to reflect on these last three years and all that has happened, how I've changed, and what I have learned. It has been a trying time. Even my testimony has been pushed to its very outer limits." I had admittedly become "very angry with God", noting, more than a year after the event, "I am still confused, and my faith somewhat shaken." I kept up the external appearances, but I was hurting on the inside. As a measure to take care of myself, in early 2014, I spoke to the stake president and asked that I be released from my calling because my mental health was not stable and I needed to heal. He was fully supportive, and I was released shortly thereafter.

There was something else important going on during 2012 through 2015 more broadly within Mormonism. With the ever-increasing prominence of the internet and social media, I began to hear more and more about "issues" in Mormon history and doctrine. General Conference talks given by apostles started—sometimes obliquely, other times more directly—to make mention of people leaving the church over these issues.

For instance, in 2012, Mormon apostle Neil L. Andersen gave a talk called "Trial of Your Faith". He noted that "there have always been a few who want to discredit the Church and to destroy faith. Today they use the Internet." He discussed how some "question their faith when they find a statement made by a Church leader decades ago that seems incongruent with our doctrine". He provided an antidote for the faithful: to immerse themselves more deeply in prayer and church service, for that is the way we overcome such trials of our faith.[2]

Dieter F. Uchtdorf, then second counselor in the church's First Presidency, gave a talk in 2013 entitled "Come, Join with Us" in which he acknowledged that people were leaving "the Church they once loved" and recognized that faithful members of the church often falsely "assume it is because they have been offended or lazy or sinful" but cautioned, "it is not that simple." He noted that "some struggle with unanswered questions about things that have been done or said in the past", and, to many people's amazement at the time, he stated, "We openly acknowledge in nearly 200 years of Church history ... there have been some things said and done that could cause people to question." Ultimately, he pleaded with people who have doubts to stay, saying, "There is yet a place for you here."[3]

In October 2015, Elder Andersen gave another talk entitled "Faith Is Not by Chance, but by Choice", in which he recognized the "important" role of "addressing honest questions" about Mormonism's past, but warned that "using our mind without our heart will not bring spiritual answers" and that "immersing oneself in persistent doubt, fueled by answers from the faithless and the unfaithful,

[2] Neil L. Andersen, "Trial of Your Faith" (182nd Semiannual General Conference of the Church of Jesus Christ of Latter-day Saints, Salt Lake City, Saturday Afternoon Session, October 6, 2012), https://www.churchofjesuschrist.org/study/general-conference/2012/10/trial-of-your-faith?lang=eng.

[3] Dieter F. Uchtdorf, "Come, Join with Us" (183rd Semiannual General Conference of the Church of Jesus Christ of Latter-day Saints, Salt Lake City, Saturday Morning Session, October 5, 2013), https://www.churchofjesuschrist.org/study/general-conference/2013/10/come-join-with-us?lang=eng.

weakens one's faith in Jesus Christ and the Restoration". He noted that "questions concerning the Prophet Joseph Smith" have "been hurled by his critics since the work began". Then he continued,

> To those of faith who, looking through the colored glasses of the 21st century, honestly question events or statements of the Prophet Joseph from nearly 200 years ago, may I share some friendly advice: For now, give Brother Joseph a break! In a future day, you will have 100 times more information than from all of today's search engines combined, and it will come from our all-knowing Father in Heaven.... I testify that Joseph Smith was a prophet of God. Settle this in your mind, and move forward![4]

During this same time, there were reports of large numbers of church members voluntarily resigning their memberships. National news outlets were reporting on these issues, including statements by Elder Marlin K. Jensen, the official Latter-day Saints church historian at the time, that attrition had accelerated greatly in the last five or ten years. Elder Jensen told a group in Logan, Utah, that never since the days of Kirtland, Ohio, had the church seen an apostasy like it was seeing now. And he admitted that the church had begun paying to achieve search-engine optimization on the internet so that its own views would be prioritized over those of its critics.[5] Outlets such as the *New York Times* and the *Washington Post* were reporting

---

[4] Neil L. Andersen, "Faith Is Not by Chance, but by Choice" (185th Semiannual General Conference of the Church of Jesus Christ of Latter-day Saints, Salt Lake City, Saturday Afternoon Session, October 4, 2015), https://www.churchofjesuschrist.org/study/general-conference/2015/10/faith-is-not-by-chance-but-by-choice?lang=eng.

[5] Peter Henderson and Kristina Cooke, "Special Report: Mormonism Besieged by the Modern Age", Reuters, January 31, 2021, https://www.reuters.com/article/us-mormonchurch/special-report-mormonism-besieged-by-the-modern-age-idUSTRE80T1CM20120131.

on high-profile excommunications, including those of the outspoken feminist and proponent of female ordination to the priesthood Kate Kelly and the host of the "Mormon Stories" podcast, John Dehlin.[6]

Beginning in 2013, the church began releasing a number of official "essays" on its website, quietly providing answers to some of the difficult questions people were apparently raising. Something was most definitely going on, and it was hard for me to ignore it all, particularly living in Salt Lake City and being in an intellectually driven profession like the law.

I considered myself firmly rooted in the faith but not naïve. Since my teenage years, I knew that there were some issues in Mormon Church history. As I mentioned earlier, I knew, for instance, that there was a connection between Mormonism's Endowment and the ceremonies of the Freemasons. I also vaguely knew that Joseph Smith had done some treasure digging when he was younger, which seemed like an odd thing for a prophet to be up to. But I believed, on the basis of Dr. Truman Madsen's writings and speeches, that he had given it up quickly—that it was simply youthful indiscretion.[7] I knew that Joseph Smith had used a "seer stone" in the translation of the *Book of Mormon*, though I didn't really know all the details. I also knew that there were supposedly varying accounts of

[6] Laurie Goodstein, "Mormons Expel Founder of Group Seeking Priesthood for Women", *New York Times*, June 24, 2014, https://www.nytimes.com /2014/06/24/us/Kate-Kelly-Mormon-Church-Excommunicates-Ordain -Women-Founder.html; Peggy Fletcher Stack, "Mormon Critic John Dehlin Is Excommunicated for 'Apostasy'", *Washington Post*, February 10, 2015, https://www.washingtonpost.com/national/religion/mormon-critic-john -dehlin-is-excommunicated-for-apostasy/2015/02/10/e26fea7a-b16a-11e4 -bf39-5560f3918d4b_story.html.

[7] Truman G. Madsen, "Joseph Smith Lecture 1: The First Vision and Its Aftermath", August 22, 1978, Brigham Young University, https://speeches .byu.edu/talks/truman-g-madsen/joseph-smith-first-vision-its-aftermath/.

the First Vision, and that Joseph had practiced polygamy (which the church would later fully embrace), but I sincerely believed God had revealed that principle to him and that the church had abandoned the practice under divine inspiration in 1890. And I also knew that Brigham Young had said all kinds of crazy things—I just wrote these off as coming in the early stages of the faith, that would obviously have some vestiges of people's preexisting beliefs that they had brought with them and that, with time, were sloughed off as the Gospel became ever more refined in its purity.

But I also began to notice an unmistakable pattern as I continued to interact with many highly educated Mormons and had private discussions about the church's teachings. I saw people starting to fall into a few defined categories. First, there were the orthodox Mormons who really just didn't have anything to say about Mormon historical, theological, or social "issues": "This is irrelevant to this month's home teaching numbers, so who cares?" Second, there were the orthodox Mormons who were into Mormon apologetics. Third, there were people who really troubled me: otherwise exceptionally faithful Mormons who had heterodox ideas. They went to church weekly, served faithfully in callings, paid their tithing, went to the temple, and so on. But they entertained ideas that seemed to me heretical, including that the *Book of Mormon* was not historical at all or that Joseph Smith's teachings on polygamy were mistaken and morally repugnant, not divine. They were highly intelligent people—and good people. And the question that troubled me was *why?* Why do these people *choose* to believe these sorts of things? Why would *anyone* choose to believe something that contradicted the church's official teaching in this way? Things were not adding up.

One day—I do not remember when or what the circumstances were, as monumental as that day ended up being—I let myself honestly ask, "What if it isn't true? What if the church isn't true? What if the reason for those failed impressions during your life, big and small, is that it was not the Holy Ghost whispering to you at all? Isn't it *possible* that that is the case? And wouldn't you *want* to know if that were the case?"

Around that time, we were preparing to move from Salt Lake City to Las Vegas for me to begin work as a law clerk for a federal judge in that area. The bishop of our ward in Salt Lake asked us to speak in sacrament meeting on whatever topics we wanted. I chose to speak on integrity. I recounted to the ward the story of a Christian martyr who, because he was a Catholic and an antagonist of the Protestant Reformers, received very little attention in the Mormon world but whose example of integrity merited our attention: Thomas More, who, as the late Justice Antonin Scalia once wryly but accurately recounted, died a martyr for a reason that "was, in the view of almost everyone at the time, a silly one.... To support the proposition that only the Bishop of Rome could bind or loose the marriage of Henry VIII."[8] That was integrity. I was emotional during the discourse in recounting his martyrdom. And for the first time, I consciously adjusted the way I presented my testimony that day to speak of things I *believed* rather than things I *knew*. And I focused on Jesus, rather than on particularities of Mormon belief that are the usual fare of testimonies. Something was rumbling beneath the surface, and I was at least attempting to have integrity.

[8] Antonin Scalia, *Scalia Speaks*, ed. Christopher J. Scalia and Edward Whelan (New York: Crown Forum, 2017), 114.

I once reflected in my journal on the fifth anniversary of my journal keeping, July 19, 2010, "on what has happened in my life in the last five years" and set my mind toward the future: "The question now becomes, what is my vision of 2015? What will I do in the next five years?" I never imagined at that time what 2015 would bring to my life.

I began to read. I read everything I could get my hands on, and I tried to be fair. I could generally spot the difference between advocacy and scholarship. A lawyer is routinely called on to engage in two different roles: advocating a position that he has been hired to defend even if he thinks it is incorrect, and counseling a client with neutral, objective advice. I had also both edited and published academic journal articles and understood the difference between an academic approach to a subject and an approach with a particular agenda. But the more I read well-written, well-researched academic treatments of Mormon history (as discussed in detail in the next chapter), the more I came to realize quickly that so much of what I had been taught—the presuppositions of my testimony—were not true at all, and that the church had, for a long time, presented a carefully curated (but not honest) version of its founding, history, and doctrine.

There was no single issue that pushed me over the edge; it was a totality of the circumstances and evidence. Like snagging your silk tie, some things just cannot be undone. And once I saw a coherent, honest, full picture of Joseph Smith and the founding and history of Mormonism, it became clear to me that whatever else the church was, it was not what it claimed to be. I was devastated, and it is hard to put into words what I felt at that time. What am I supposed to make of my life? My career choices? My marriage? How will I raise my children? How will I discuss this with my wife, my parents, my friends? What do I do about the church? Do I keep going? Do I tell other people what I've found? Is God even real? How do I know what is right and what is wrong anymore? If the church has been wrong in the past on social questions that it presented as doctrinal and official teaching, is the church right or wrong about the social questions it is addressing now? Such questions unsettled my mind and, frankly, scourged my soul. But on reflection, I concluded, painfully and regretfully, with piercing sorrow—the church wasn't true. The testimony on which I had based so much of my life was illusory.

6

The Dark Night of the Soul, Part II

TO COVER IN A SINGLE CHAPTER issues on which multiple
books have been written is not possible. Nor does it seem
particularly useful to recount all the problems the traditional Mormon account of Mormonism's history and
doctrine raises. Readers interested in learning more can
turn to a suggested reading list in the appendix, although
that list is itself not sufficiently inclusive. But for our purposes here, I will summarize at a high level of generality
the nature of some of the serious historical problems in
Mormonism that led me to conclude that the religion's
claims were false.

I claim no originality in the way I describe these various historical matters. Nor by the inclusion of any one
example do I mean to communicate that this or that fact
or discovery was crucial to the unwinding of my faith. As
I mentioned earlier, it was the totality. But I hope that
through these examples, I can paint the outlines of that
totality, so that the reader can understand just how different the Mormonism of history turned out to be from the
Mormonism on which my testimony was based, and why,
in the state I was in at the time, it proved so convincing as
to require me to leave the Mormon faith in which I had
been raised and in which I had so ardently believed.

Folk Magic and the Founding of Mormonism

In 1985, an explosive scandal broke out in Salt Lake City, Utah. Mark Hofmann—a young man renowned for his uncanny ability to locate rare historical documents, particularly rare Mormon historical documents—was injured by a car bomb. Incidentally, his injuries occurred just a day after two other people (Steven Christensen and Kathy Sheets) had been killed by two separate bombs. The headlines across the country soon broke as authorities discovered that Hofmann had in fact been a forger. A series of events had been threatening to unmask his scheme, and he turned to murder to try to cover his tracks. Not long before his fraud unraveled, Hofmann was involved in the "discovery" of what was known as the "Salamander Letter"—a letter supposedly written by early Mormon leader Martin Harris, in which Harris recounted the circumstances under which Joseph Smith discovered the golden plates, but with facts and details completely foreign to the traditional Mormon account that the church taught its members and the world. The relevant text of the (fraudulent) letter read:

Dear Sir

Your letter of yesterday is received & I hasten to answer as fully as I can—Joseph Smith Jr first come to my notice in the year 1824 in the summer of that year I contracted with his father to build a fence on my property in the corse of that work I aproach Joseph & ask how it is in a half day you put up what requires your father & 2 brothers a full day working together he says I have not been with out assistance but can not say more only you better find out the next day I take the older Smith by the arm & he says Joseph can see any thing he wishes by looking at a stone Joseph often sees Spirits here with great kettles of coin money it was Spirits who brought up rock because Joseph made no attempt on their money I latter dream I converse with spirits which let me count their money when I awake I have in my hand a dollar coin which I take for a sign Joseph describes what I seen in every particular says he the spirits are greived so I through back the dollar In the fall of the year 1827 I hear Joseph found a gold bible I take Joseph aside & he says it is true I found it 4 years ago with my stone but only just got it because of the enchantment the old spirit come to me 3 times in the same dream & says dig up the gold but when I take it up the next morning the spirit transfigured himself from a white salamander in the bottom of the hole & struck me 3 times & held the treasure & would not let me have it because I lay it down to cover over the hole when the spirit says do not lay it down Joseph says when can I have it the spirit says one year from to day if you obay me look to the stone after a few days he looks the spirit says bring your brother Alvin Joseph says he is dead shall I bring what remains but the spirit is gone Joseph goes to get the gold bible but the spirit says you did not bring your brother you can not have it look to the stone Joseph looks but can not see who to bring the spirit says I tricked you again look to the stone Joseph looks & sees his wife on the 22d day of Sept 1827 they get the gold bible. . . .

Yours Respectfully
Martin Harris[1]

Mormon leaders—along with most commentators and historians involved—were fooled by Hofmann's forgery. The church made some official announcements about the letter

[1] "The Salamander Letter", *Los Angeles Times*, March 29, 1987, https://www.latimes.com/archives/la-xpm-1987-03-29-tm-793-story.html.

in 1984 and 1985, and a number of Mormon apologists (as well as Mormon apostles) leaped into damage-control mode to explain to members the bizarre contents of the letter and to try to reconcile them with the traditional story of the Angel Moroni. Mormon apostle Dallin Oaks, for instance, gave a speech in which he advanced the far-fetched theory that the word "salamander" was another word for "angel" at that time.[2]

Luckily for everyone involved, Hofmann botched his bombing spree and was brought to justice, admitting his forgeries. Yet since that time, when the church has discussed people leaving the faith because of historical discoveries about early Mormonism, it has frequently been able to frame the "Salamander Letter" controversy to its advantage: a cautionary tale about trusting in historical materials that paint a scandalous picture of Joseph Smith.

For example, in his October 2012 General Conference discourse that I mentioned earlier, Elder Neil Andersen recounted the "Salamander Letter" controversy. Although he did not mention it by name, he discussed an event in "1985" reported in *Time* magazine involving supposedly "new information" threatening to "destroy the Mormon Church"—"a recently discovered letter, supposedly written by Martin Harris, that conflicted with Joseph Smith's account of the finding of the Book of Mormon plates". As Elder Andersen explains it, some members of the church tragically left "over the document" when only "a few months later experts discovered (and the forger confessed) that the letter was a complete fraud." Thus, Elder Andersen's talk warns those who have doubts about the church, using this example, that

---

[2] Dallin H. Oaks, "Reading Church History" (CES Doctrine and Covenants Symposium, Brigham Young University, August 16, 1985), https://scott woodward.org/old/Talks/html/Oaks,%20Dallin%20H/OaksDH_Reading ChurchHistory.html.

"some of the information about the Church, no matter how convincing, is just not true."[3]

As I began to read more and more about Mormon history, I discovered that there was a reason that Mormon leaders and many church historians reluctantly accepted the authenticity of the "Salamander Letter" and other similar letters Hofmann forged at the time. It was not merely Hofmann's talents in matching nineteenth-century paper and ink or matching handwriting or pioneer diction. Rather, the reason the "Salamander Letter" proved so convincing was that the description of Joseph engaged in magical treasure quests with a jealous trickster guardian spirit that could shape-shift, cast enchantments on him and the golden plates, and demand Joseph's participation in a years-long ritual magic puzzle was in fact the context of the early accounts of the coming forth of the *Book of Mormon*. Many church leaders and historians knew this but kept that narrative carefully obscured from church members, minimizing the true nature of the early accounts.

The documentation, from friendly and unfriendly sources alike, uniformly and clearly shows that Joseph Smith, his parents, his siblings, his friends, his associates, and even some of his enemies were steeped in the nineteenth-century folk-magic traditions of the Northeastern United States. The *Book of Mormon* is inextricably tied to those practices and beliefs. Joseph's family members possessed magical daggers and parchments with kabbalistic spells and incantations on them. They used enchanted amulets. They used "divining rods" that they would ask questions and that would twitch up or down to give answers to them, about everything from locating water to finding mystical buried treasures to receiving revelations from God. Early Mormon figure Oliver Cowdery was a practicing rodsman. A purported revelation from God through Joseph Smith to Oliver Cowdery, published originally in the *Book of Commandments*, spoke approvingly of Oliver's "gift, which is the gift of working with the rod; behold it has told you things: behold there is no other power save God, that can cause this rod of nature, to work in your hands, for it is the work of God; and therefore whatsoever you shall ask me to tell you by that means, that will I grant unto you, that you shall know."[4] That revelation was later retroactively edited to refer instead, as it does now in contemporary editions of *Doctrine and Covenants*, to "the gift of Aaron"—an attempt to obscure the folk-magic elements of Mormonism's founding and simultaneously give a Judeo-Christian veneer to the whole affair.

Historians, both Mormon and non-Mormon, accept that Joseph Smith was a well-known village magician, whose occult services for finding buried treasure and other lost objects were sought out during a period of his life that lasted about eight years—the same period in which he later claimed visits from an angel telling him of the location of the *Book of Mormon*, his prophetic calling, and the need for a restoration of Christ's true church. Joseph's treasure-seeking career followed a settled pattern—so settled that Benjamin Franklin had described it in uncannily accurate satire more than a century earlier:

There are among us great Numbers of honest Artificers and labouring People, who fed with a vain Hope

---

[4] Joseph Smith, *A Book of Commandments, for the Government of the Church of Christ, Organized According to Law, on the 6th of April, 1830* (Zion: W. W. Phelps & Co., 1833), chap. 7, verse 3.

of growing suddenly rich, neglect their Business, almost
to the ruining of themselves and Families, and voluntarily endure abundance of Fatigue in a fruitless Search
after Imaginary hidden treasure. They wander thro' the
Woods and Bushes by Day, to discover the Marks and
Signs; at Midnight they repair to the hopeful Spot with
Spades and Pickaxes; full of Expectation, they labour violently, trembling at the same Time, in every Joint, thro'
Fear of certain malicious Demons who are said to haunt
and guard such Places. At length a mighty hole is dug, and
perhaps several Cart-loads of Earth thrown out; but alas,
no Cag or Iron Pot is found! No Seaman's Chest cram'd
with Spanish Pistoles, or weighty Pieces of Eight! Then
they conclude, that, thro some Mistake in the Procedure,
some rash Word spoke, or some Rule of Art neglected,
the Guardian Spirit had Power to sink it deeper into the
Earth and convey it out of their Reach. Yet when a Man
is once thus infatuated, he is so far from being discour-
aged by ill Success, that he is rather animated to double
his Industry, and will try again and again in a Hundred
Different Places, in Hopes at last of meeting with some
lucky Hit, that shall at once sufficiently reward him for all
his Expence of Time and Labour.[5]

Numerous contemporaneous sources indicate that Joseph
Smith's treasure-quest exploits followed this pattern nearly
to a tee. He obtained one of his favorite seer stones during
what was likely a treasure quest, but was ostensibly a well-
digging job, with or for Willard Chase, whose sister Sally
Chase was also a reputed seer in the community. Like
Sally, with whom Joseph competed for followers and cli-
ents, Joseph would take the stone, place it inside a hat,
stick his face in the hat, and, peeping into the stone, tell his

[5] Carl van Doren, ed., *Benjamin Franklin and Jonathan Edwards: Selections from Their Writings* (New York: Charles Scribner and Sons, 1920), 25.

customers in vivid detail where to find buried Indian treasures or Spanish silver mines guarded by malevolent spirits.

He would also give magical instructions to his customers,
to be followed precisely, which would bind the treasure in
place and ward off the guardian spirit so the treasure diggers
could obtain it. Joseph's family's magical dagger was used
in the ritual magic required before treasure digging (draw-
ing circles around the treasure and the like). His patrons—
frequently true believers, to be sure—often reported striking
the tops of treasure chests with their shovels, yet they always
added that, somehow, the treasure narrowly eluded them,
slipping further into the earth just ahead of the glances of
their picks and shovels. Joseph would then inform them
of why the quest had failed: someone had made a misstep,
failed to keep sacred silence, mispronounced an incantation,
or otherwise erred in the required magical practices, thus
permitting the treasures to slip into the earth beyond their
grasp.

Taught by his father, Joseph Sr., Joseph began using a
dowsing rod as early as the age of eleven, in 1817, and
obtained his first seer stone by 1819. Joseph found his most
famous seer stone in 1822, and from 1823 through 1827
engaged in numerous treasure quests, each following the
prescribed patterns of folk-magic belief outlined above.
Perhaps unsurprisingly, however, Joseph's vocation was
illegal in New York. A misdemeanor statute existed at the
time "for Apprehending and Punishing Disorderly Persons", aimed at, among others, "all jugglers, and all persons
pretending to have skill in physiognomy, palmistry, or like
crafty science, or pretending to tell fortunes, or to discover
where lost goods may be found."[6] In 1826, Joseph was

---

[6] William P. Van Ness and John Woodworth, *Laws of the State of New-York,
Revised and Passed at the Thirty-Sixth Session of the Legislature* (Albany: H.C.
Southwick & Co., 1813), 1:114.

apprehended, pursuant to this statute, in a case the judge called *People v. Joseph Smith the Glass Looker.*

Historians are divided on the question of whether Joseph was ultimately convicted of violating this law, because the original court proceedings did not survive, but only the trial bills and several mildly differing accounts of the trial testimony, requiring historians to piece together the events. But whether Joseph was technically convicted or not is hardly the point and ultimately a question of historical trivia. The real takeaway is that friendly and unfriendly witnesses alike testified to Joseph's career as a "seer"; the only difference is that some people honestly believed in his talents, while others believed they were fraudulent.

This event in 1826—along with an emotional confrontation with his father-in-law, Isaac Hale, over Joseph's scurrilous profession and his having married Isaac's daughter Emma without permission—seems to have impacted Joseph. Around this time, 1827, one of his ongoing treasure quests that had begun in 1823 began to evolve more and more from a treasure quest into a religious project.

Early accounts of the golden plates from which Joseph Smith purportedly produced the *Book of Mormon* differ from the later 1838 account (eight years after the Mormon Church was officially founded) in that they present Joseph's story in its proper magical, treasure-quest context. The later accounts present it in slightly more recognizable religious terms. For instance, using that 1838 account, Mormons are taught that somewhat out of the blue, Joseph Smith was worrying about his sins on the night of September 21, 1823, when the angel Moroni appeared to him to tell him of a work God had for him, revealing the presence of golden plates and telling Joseph they were an ancient record of the true Gospel as taught to ancient inhabitants of the Americas. The angel quoted Bible verses, according to this later account, and, as Joseph would tell the story,

"While he was conversing with me about the plates, the vision was opened to my mind that I could see the place where the plates were deposited, and that so clearly and distinctly that I knew the place again when I visited it."[7] Yet early accounts, including one from Martin Harris, state that Joseph Smith found the plates by gazing into the seer stone he found on the Chase property, not by having been given a "vision" from an "angel" in the Judeo-Christian sense, as Mormons think of the event today.

Similarly, while the Mormon Church and its defenders today will frequently connect the date of Moroni's first visit in 1823 with the celebration of the Jewish feast of Tabernacles (and the September 22, 1827, date when Joseph finally received the plates with the feast of Trumpets), those are later-imposed Judeo-Christian glosses, which leave out the much more likely reason for Joseph's assertions about important events happening on those days: they were astrologically significant to Joseph, who took numerous important actions throughout his life based on astrology.

As another example, in Joseph's 1838 account, Mormons are taught that Joseph was instructed to go to the Hill Cumorah the day after this vision, and that he "made an attempt to take [the plates] out, but was forbidden by the messenger, and was again informed that the time for bringing them forth had not yet arrived, neither would it, until four years from that time".[8] Rather, Joseph claimed that the angel said that he "should come to that place precisely in one year from that time, and that he would there meet with me, and that I should continue to do so until the time should come for obtaining the plates".

---

[7] Joseph Smith, *History of the Church of Jesus Christ of Latter-day Saints* (Salt Lake City: Deseret Book, 1978), 1:42.

[8] Smith, *History*, 1:53.

Mormons are taught that Joseph did as was commanded and "went at the end of each year, and at each time ... found the same messenger there, and received instruction and intelligence from him at each of [their] interviews, respecting what the Lord was going to do, and how and in what manner his kingdom was to be conducted in the last days".[9]

But early accounts again present the events in a different, magical, context. Those accounts often describe a "spirit", rather than an "angel", and that spirit was reported to have acted in a markedly hostile manner—more a Rumpelstiltskin than a Gabriel. One of Joseph's neighbors stated that "when [Joseph] took the plates there was something down near the box that looked some [sic] like a toad that rose up into a man which forbid him to take the plates."[10] Willard Chase swore in an 1833 affidavit that upon Joseph's first attempt to recover the plates, "he saw in the box something like a toad, which assumed the appearance of a man, and struck him on the side of his head." Joseph then got the plates, set them down, and turned around, and the plates had magically reappeared in the box in the ground. He tried again, "and the spirit struck him again, and knocked him three or four rods" (fifteen to twenty-two feet), proceeding to give Joseph instructions to come back a year later with his brother Alvin to get the plates.[11] Oliver Cowdery reported that Joseph was "prevented from obtaining the gold treasure by a thrice-repeated shock" from the spirit.[12]

---

[9] Smith, *History*, 1:53–54.

[10] Dan Vogel, *Early Mormon Documents* (Salt Lake City: Signature Books, 1998), 2:137. On the "spirit", see Dan Vogel, *The Making of a Prophet* (Salt Lake City: Signature Books, 2004), 45.

[11] E.D. Howe, *Mormonism Unveiled* (Painesville, 1834), 242.

[12] D. Michael Quinn, *Early Mormonism and the Magic World View* (Salt Lake City: Signature Books, 1998), 162.

Alvin died shortly thereafter, leading to a bizarre incident involving rumors of Alvin's body being exhumed (it likely was not) and the spirit telling Joseph he needed to bring another man with him later. Reports indicate that Joseph chose his fellow reputed seer Samuel Lawrence to accompany him. Lawrence, when gazing into his seer stone, reported not just seeing the golden plates as Joseph had seen, but doing him one better: he also saw a pair of "spectacles" (that is, seer stones set like glasses).[13] Joseph could not see them at first, but then looked again into Lawrence's stone and saw them, too. They did not obtain the treasure on that date, however. The golden plates were supposedly "recovered" in 1827 by Joseph, who by this time had been instructed to have his new wife, Emma, accompany him. Using a black horse and carriage and clad entirely in black as per a requirement given to him by the spirit and a common magical requirement of treasure quests of the time, Joseph claimed to be successful on this last attempt, recovering the plates and the set of "spectacles".

Joseph is reported to have continued treasure digging after that point as well. According to Martin Harris, "after Joe had found the plates", Martin, Joseph Sr., and Joseph Jr., all "took some tools to go to the hill (Cumorah) and hunt for some more boxes ... and indeed we found [one]. We got quite excited about it", Harris reported, and "dug quite carefully around it", but when they were "ready to take it up ... behold, by some unseen power, it slipped back into the hill."[14] He claimed that they "glanced" the stone chest, breaking off one corner, before it slipped further into the earth just outside their reach, as such treasures invariably did.

[13] Quinn, *Early Mormonism*, 162.
[14] Quinn, *Early Mormonism*, 61.

Numerous other folk-magic details infuse the story of the *Book of Mormon*, nearly all of which were, for a long time, omitted by the church in its official histories or, if not omitted, obscured or minimized in one way or another. I had heard tidbits about Joseph Smith's treasure digging when I was younger. Indeed, Truman Madsen, in the lecture series that had been so important to me, conceded that Joseph admitted it had happened, but wrote it off as a minor indiscretion insignificant to his life. It became increasingly clear to me that the reality was much different. Certainly, this was not the story I was told about Joseph Smith, nor was I told as a missionary to teach anything like it to prospective converts.

Researching this topic made it clear that the folk magic beginnings of Mormonism were inextricably intertwined with the "restoration" of the Gospel, and it grew increasingly clear that Joseph's magical (and to my mind, fraudulent) treasure-seeking exploits were the actual origin of my religion. After all, when Joseph Smith then began to produce the *Book of Mormon*, he did it in an awfully familiar way—not as I had always been taught, but by placing the seer stone found on the Chase property into his top hat, placing his face into the hat, and "seeing" the text of the *Book of Mormon* appear in the stone, which he would then dictate, generally without the plates even being in the room.

Why Joseph's magical treasure quests began to take on a religious context is open to reasonable speculation. His family's dire financial circumstances, his trouble with the law for searching for treasure, his confrontation with Isaac Hale over Emma, and other circumstances are individually and collectively plausible explanations. But, in context, and along with all the other evidence, the explanation put forward by the church and various Mormon apologists—that Joseph Smith was a prophet called by

God, even if that calling was gradually revealed through Joseph's immediate cultural context—is just not believable. If it were, it would be the story Mormon missionaries teach openly and outright to prospective converts, and people would be converting and bearing testimony about the realities of the powers of magical stones. But it is not. And it was not the foundation on which my testimonial experience had been premised.

The Book of Mormon*'s Translation and Its Contents*

Learning more about the *Book of Mormon* itself helped provide further context for the unwinding of my faith.

As alluded to above, to this day, the church frequently depicts Joseph Smith sitting ponderously over a set of open golden plates before him, studying their characters and dictating their contents to a scribe seated nearby. Sometimes he is even featured with the Urim and Thummim, an apparatus that looks like a set of glasses, attached to a breast plate he is wearing. The depictions give the impression that Joseph looked at the characters in the *Book of Mormon*, and by God's power, either directly or through the Urim and Thummim, translated those characters and dictated the words to his scribe. That is certainly how I was taught the process happened.

But that is not what happened. Accounts of the production of the *Book of Mormon* state that Joseph took his brown seer stone discovered on the Chase property, just as he did in seeking for treasure, placed it in his top hat, and buried his face inside, and the words of the *Book of Mormon* would appear verbatim on the stone, which Joseph would then dictate to his scribes. To my astonishment, I learned that by many accounts, the plates were generally not even in the room when Joseph would do this (only a few accounts indicate that *sometimes* the plates were in the room, but they would be covered up by a napkin—Joseph was not even looking at them). The entire text of the *Book of Mormon* as it was originally printed in 1830 appeared by this process.

The references to the Urim and Thummim used appear to be later religious glosses referring to Joseph's seer stone (the Urim and Thummim were divination stones referred to in the Old Testament). Indeed, the very existence of this set of "spectacles" in the story of the *Book of Mormon* is sheer historical accident. Samuel Lawrence claimed to see them in his peep stone, requiring Joseph to account for them from that moment forward. But the more time passed, the more and more the origins of the *Book of Mormon* began to stray from their folk-magic context and began to take on the trappings of a pseudo-Christian religion. The realization that Joseph Smith's "gift and power of God" by which he translated the *Book of Mormon* used the same means, exactly, by which he guided people for money on numerous failed treasure quests and for which he may well have been convicted of committing a form of fraud in 1826 certainly cast the *Book of Mormon* in a new light for me.

There was also, of course, the matter of the book's contents, which are decidedly religious, rather than principally or even secondarily occupied with folk magic. The church presents the *Book of Mormon*, as Joseph Smith himself said it was, as the "most correct of any book on earth",[15] lauding its deep spirituality and showing it off as affirmative evidence of Joseph Smith's prophetic calling. How, after all, could Joseph, a young man of little education who,

[15] Smith, *History*, 4:461.

according to later accounts by Emma, could barely scratch out his own name, produce such a "marvelous work and a wonder", especially in so short a time period—"sixty-five working days", between April 7 and June 30, 1829?[16] It turned out that the book was maybe not so marvelous as I had been taught.

The *Book of Mormon*'s major textual source, as it happens, is a 1769 edition of the King James Bible. As one scholar reports, the *Book of Mormon* contains twenty-six full chapters of that 1769 edition of the King James Bible, and quotations from many other verses still.[17] That same scholar reports that of the over three hundred names in the *Book of Mormon*, about two-thirds are taken either directly from the Bible or are rhyming or spelling variations of biblical names (coincidentally, Joseph possessed a Bible that contained a handy table of all the names used in the Bible).[18]

From Alma the Younger's conversion story (see Saint Paul's conversion) to Nephi's beheading of Laban (see Judith and Holofernes, not to mention David and Goliath) to the lengthy verbatim quotations of Old and New Testament texts, the Bible permeates the *Book of Mormon* in specific language, overarching patterns, and general motifs and story lines. *Book of Mormon*'s prophecies of the details of Jesus' name, birthplace, and ministry are contained in astounding accuracy and are suspiciously clearer than the prophecies of the Old Testament on which early

---

[16] John W. Welch, "How Long Did It Take Joseph Smith to Translate the Book of Mormon?", *Ensign*, January 1988, https://www.churchofjesuschrist.org /study/ensign/1988/01/i-have-a-question/how-long-did-it-take-joseph-smith -to-translate-the-book-of-mormon?lang=eng.

[17] Grant Palmer, *An Insider's View of Mormon Origins* (Salt Lake City: Signature Books, 2002), 83.

[18] Palmer, *Mormon Origins*, 70n2.

Christians relied for their messianic understanding of Jesus. After I read scholarly analyses, the *Book of Mormon*'s reliance on the Bible became patently obvious to me from its first page to its last, and I felt embarrassed for having ever entertained common church-produced explanations of the presence of those texts in the *Book of Mormon* (for example, God wanted people to receive the text of the *Book of Mormon* in familiar language, so he inspired Joseph to use those words and phrases).

Joseph's own life also likely provided material for the *Book of Mormon*. Folk magic makes its appearances in Helaman chapter 13's discussion of "slippery" treasures and the defense of seer stones and their use in translation in Mosiah chapters 8 and 28 and Alma chapter 37. The prophet Lehi's vision of a "tree of life" in 1 Nephi bears an uncanny resemblance to a vision Joseph Smith Sr. had in 1811 and had recounted to the family. The entire premise of the *Book of Mormon* (a lost branch of the Tribes of Israel navigates to the Americas and becomes the ancestors of Native Americans) bears a strong resemblance to those same Indian origin stories in Rev. Ethan Smith's *A View of the Hebrews*, published in 1825 (Rev. Smith was Oliver Cowdery's family pastor in Vermont). The list could go on.

I also learned of the anachronisms in the *Book of Mormon*, such as mentions of silk, steel, chariots, elephants, and horses. Preaching styles and crowd reactions characteristic of nineteenth-century Protestant revival camp meetings are present in many instances. And the book is noticeably geared toward answering several specific religious controversies of the Protestant Northeast of Joseph's time. As contemporary minister Alexander Campbell commented in his review of the *Book of Mormon*, the book discusses "every error and almost every truth discussed in New York for the last ten years ... decid[ing] all the great controversies" of the time, including "infant baptism, ordination, the trinity, regeneration, repentance, justification, the fall of man, the atonement, transubstantiation, fasting penance, church government, religious experience, the call to the ministry, the general resurrection, eternal punishment, who may baptize, and even the questions of free masonry, republican government and the rights of man".[19]

The original text of the 1830 *Book of Mormon*, later cleaned up by the church, is full of grammar typical of that era, further showing it to be a product of its time (especially in light of the historical accounts that Joseph dictated the words God made appear on the seer stone). One source has compiled every textual change the *Book of Mormon* has undergone, just shy of four thousand, including the many instances of grammatical tidying up. Among these are the use of the word "was" when "were" should be used, "is" when "are" should be used, "a" preceding participles, and "for" before infinitives, for example:

- "Adam and Eve, which was our first parents"
- "all these things of which I have spoken, was done"
- "And great was the covenants of the Lord"
- "because it were easy to guard them"
- "And whoredoms is an abomination before me"
- "As I was a journeying to see a very near kindred"
- "as Ammon and Lamoni was a journeying thither"
- "they did prepare for to meet them"[20]

---

[19] Alexander Campbell, *Delusions: An Analysis of the Book of Mormon; with an Examination of Its Internal and External Evidences, and a Refutation of Its Pretences to Divine Authority* (Boston: Benjamin H. Greene, 1832), 13.

[20] Jerald and Sandra Tanner, *3,913 Changes in the Book of Mormon* (Salt Lake City: Utah Lighthouse Ministries, 1996), introduction.

Such folksy diction litters the original text of the *Book of Mormon* and helps put the book in its proper context for what it really was—a largely derivative nineteenth-century work of frontier American religious thought.

But how could Joseph have accomplished this? Mormon Church defenders routinely raise this objection, even though it is also readily answerable. To begin with, there is no reason to suppose that the burden of proof about the historicity of the *Book of Mormon* lies with those who believe it to be a product of the nineteenth century rather than with those who believe it is ancient. The contrary presupposition of many defenders of the *Book of Mormon* gets things exactly backwards. Nor would it follow, in any event, that the burden of proof with respect to the book's historicity also encompasses a requirement of detailing how the text came to be. For example, if I found a piece of paper on the sidewalk outside my home right now that told a story in English about how the people of ancient Egypt had the internet and spoke French and listened to the Beatles, there is no burden whatsoever on me, as a part of my own argument that the text is not authentically historical, to explain to someone *where* the text came from, *who* wrote it, and *whether* more than one person wrote it. Indeed, even my complete inability to answer any of those questions with certainty would not detract from the simple conclusion that the text was not ancient. Personally, I didn't and still don't really care how Joseph Smith produced the *Book of Mormon*. There are many theories, nearly all of which are more plausible than the explanation given by Mormonism. How did Joseph Smith accurately see a feather in the ground through his seer stone (as has been attested to by some of his treasure-quest customers) that he was then able to dig up as proof of his talents? No one knows for certain, because we do not have any direct evidence, but I am reasonably confident the answer is not faith-promoting. Based on the totality of evidence, I could confidently conclude that the *Book of Mormon* was not what it claimed to be without having to explain what, in fact, it was.

At the same time, it is not overly difficult to sketch reasonable ideas about how the *Book of Mormon* was produced. Reciting texts committed to memory seems to be something Joseph had practiced. One witness at his 1826 trial testified that he went to see Joseph to judge whether "he possessed the skill that he professed to have", at which point Joseph "laid a Book open upon a White Cloth, and proposed looking through another stone which was white and transparent; held the stone to the candle, turned his back to [the] book and read".[21] And Joseph Smith may have technically dictated the text of the *Book of Mormon* in sixty-five working days, but he had years to hone his story. He supposedly recovered the golden plates in September 1827 yet did not begin "translating" them until the following spring. As Mormons well know, Joseph produced a 116-page manuscript that was then lost, and he took a significant amount of time off before starting again in April 1829. In all, that was more than enough time for Joseph to plan out the story line of the *Book of Mormon*. Joseph Smith's ability to produce the *Book of Mormon* Mormon given his gifts, charisma, improvisational skills, and memory and the literary resources available to him (all well documented) is sufficient to explain reasonably that the *Book of Mormon* is not what the Church presents it as, which was all that was necessary for me.

---

[21] "Appendix: Docket Entry, 20 March 1826 [*State of New York v. JS–A*]", Joseph Smith Papers, Church History Library of the Church of Jesus Christ of Latter-day Saints in Salt Lake City, Utah, https://www.josephsmithpapers.org /paper-summary/appendix-docket-entry-20-march-1826-people-v-js/1.

In the early twentieth century, Mormon seventy Elder
B. H. Roberts undertook a critical examination of the
Book of Mormon at the request of Mormon apostle James
E. Talmage, who had received a letter from a young man
from Salina, Utah, positing five serious difficulties with the
Book of Mormon. Roberts ultimately produced three written works, totaling over 250 pages, considering problems
with the *Book of Mormon*, its likely sources, and the history
of its production. Roberts concluded, "There can be no
doubt" that possessed "of a vividly strong, creative imagination," along with "common knowledge" of his time
about the beliefs of American Indians, "supplemented by
such a work as Ethan Smith's *View of the Hebrews*", it was
"possible for [Joseph] to create a book such as the Book
of Mormon".[22]

His textual criticisms were honest but withering. The
narratives of the *Book of Mormon*, he wrote, evinced a
"certain lack of perspective in the things the book relates
as history that points quite clearly to an undeveloped
mind as their origin".[23] His comparison of the various
"Anti-Christs" of the *Book of Mormon* (Jacob, Sherem, and
Korihor), and his ultimate conclusion about them, was
stinging: "In addition to the striking parallelism" between
the anti-Christs of the *Book of Mormon* and "the strong
implication that they have their origin in one mind", he
emphasized the "rawness" and "amateurishness" of the
theology presented by stories involving these characters.
Roberts asked:

Does it not carry with it the proof that it is the work of
a pious youth dealing with the very common place stock

[22] B. H. Roberts, *Studies of the Book of Mormon*, ed. Brigham Madsen, 2nd ed.
(Salt Lake City: Signature Books, 1992), 250.
[23] Roberts, *Studies of the Book of Mormon*, 251.

arguments clumsily put together for the belief in the existence of God[?] ... I shall hold that what is here presented
illustrates sufficiently the matter taken in hand by referring
to them [the *Book of Mormon* Anti-Christs], namely that
they are all of one breed and brand; so nearly alike that one
mind is the author of them, and that a young and undeveloped, but piously inclined mind. The evidence, I sor-
rowfully submit, points to Joseph Smith as their creator. It
is difficult to believe that they are the product of history.[24]

Difficult indeed.

The Book of Abraham *and Translation More Generally*

Coming to grips with the details of how Joseph Smith produced the *Book of Mormon* placed the historical facts surrounding the production of another Mormon scripture—the
Book of Abraham—in a different light and recontextualized
my understanding of Joseph Smith's claims to have translated ancient records "by the gift and power of God" (*Book
of Mormon*, title page). It was not good.

In the summer of 1835, a traveling exhibit of Egyptian mummies and papyri came to Kirtland, Ohio, where
Joseph Smith and the Mormon Church had gathered.
Unbeknownst to Joseph, or to anyone in the world at that
time, the papyri accompanying the mummies were ordinary Egyptian funerary texts. Joseph took an immediate
interest in them, which is unsurprising, given that the language in which the prophets of the *Book of Mormon* supposedly inscribed their history onto the golden plates was

---

[24] Roberts, *Studies of the Book of Mormon*, 271.

"Reformed Egyptian". Joseph Smith bought the exhibit from Michael Chandler for $2,400. Flash forward to 1842, when Joseph Smith began publishing excerpts, claiming the papyri contained a record of the biblical patriarch Abraham. Indeed, the book begins, "The Book of Abraham / Translated from the Papyrus / by Joseph Smith / A Translation of some ancient Records that have fallen into our hands from the catacombs of Egypt. The writings of Abraham while he was in Egypt, called the Book of Abraham, written by his own hand, upon papyrus."[25]

The *Book of Abraham* teaches some of Mormonism's key doctrines about the preexistence of spirits, the Plan of Salvation, and the plurality of gods. Published with the book were several woodcuts of the papyri, with numbered footnotes purporting to give translations of selected images and characters. The text itself refers to the images. Most famously, one of the images depicts Abraham lying on an altar, about to be sacrificed with a knife by an idolatrous priest, while a bird-like figure (said by Joseph to represent an angel) swoops down to rescue Abraham. The text of the book says, in chapter 1, verse 12, "that you may have a knowledge of this altar, I will refer you to the representation at the commencement of this record"—that is, the woodcuts taken from the papyrus. Mormons are all familiar with these pictures, as they appear to this day in their canonical copies of the *Book of Abraham*.

It is well documented that Joseph Smith represented to people that he had translated these papyri, by God's power, from Egyptian into English. When Josiah Quincy—future mayor of Boston—made a visit to meet Joseph Smith, he was shown the mummies, and Joseph Smith is recorded as having told him a number of details about the mummies

[25] *Abraham* 1.

and the papyri. He reportedly told Quincy that one of the mummies "was Pharaoh Necho, King of Egypt!" and, pointing to the papyri, informed him, "That is the handwriting of Abraham, the Father of the Faithful."[26]

After Joseph Smith's death, most Mormons trekked westward, but the papyri stayed behind in Illinois. They were believed by many to have been lost in Chicago's great fire of 1871. But given the woodcuts published in the *Book of Abraham*, it did not take long for actual Egyptologists to raise eyebrows at the claimed "translation". Beginning in 1861 through the early twentieth century, a number of scholars, at times in unflattering tones, pointed out that Joseph Smith's "translation" was wrong, appeared made up, and was filled with anachronisms. Things changed markedly in the fall of 1967 when the papyri were discovered in New York and donated back to the church. The papyri were confirmed to be the same ones purchased and used by Joseph Smith, including the images on which the woodcuts in the *Book of Abraham* are based. The eleven papyri fragments were translated by Egyptologists. The fragments have nothing to do with Abraham or even Abrahamic religion whatsoever.

Joseph Smith's "translation" was not just wrong, it was embarrassingly so. The papyri are ordinary Egyptian funerary texts dating far too late to have been written by Abraham. Some of the images as they appear in Mormon Scriptures were doctored from the original papyri. That is, neither Facsimile 1 nor 2, as they appear in the printed *Book of Abraham*, is a faithful copy of the images on the papyri, which are missing pieces—pieces that someone (either Joseph Smith or someone under his direction) filled

---

[26] Robert K. Ritner, *The Joseph Smith Egyptian Papyri: A Complete Edition* (Salt Lake City: Signature Books, 2013), 2.

in with pencil drawings, substantially altering the images. For example, a figure presented as having a human head and a knife in his hand in the *Book of Abraham* should actually have a dog's head and no knife at all (because the image is not of a human sacrifice on an altar).

What's more, just a year or so before the rediscovery of the papyri in 1967, researchers obtained a leaked copy of a restricted document that had been long hidden in the church's vaults. The document was called the "Egyptian Grammar and Alphabet". This document shows the process by which Joseph created the text of the *Book of Abraham*, taking a character from the papyri and extrapolating from a single character lines and lines of text, then moving to the next character and so on. At the time I discovered this, it still seemed that the church was not quite ready to own up to the fact that these documents were used in the production of the *Book of Abraham*, but by the time I wrote this book, the Joseph Smith Papers Project—an official historical church publication—seems to have accepted it.

Much as with the *Book of Mormon*, many researchers have persuasively reconstructed the sources on which the *Book of Abraham* relied, in addition to Joseph's own theological and historical imagination. The writings of Flavius Josephus provided some of the influence, a book that Oliver Cowdery had in his possession at the time the "translation" of the *Book of Abraham* began. As one scholar has written, "The primary source for chapters 2, 4, and 5 ... is Genesis 1, 2, 11 ... and 12. Sixty-six out of seventy-seven verses in this section of Abraham (86 percent) are quotations or close paraphrases of [King James Bible] wording."[27] The "astronomical phrases and concepts" throughout the book are very similar to those

[27] Palmer, *Mormon Origins*, 19.

found in the 1816 book by Thomas Taylor, *The Six Books of Proclus on the Theology of Plato*. And the 1830 edition of Thomas Dick's *Philosophy of a Future State* also appears to have been influential, another book in Joseph Smith's possession at the time.[28]

As I read through the church's official essay on this topic, as well as some Mormon responses, I found them desperate. Perhaps the most disturbing of all explanations I read was the one the church may currently be settling on: the so-called "catalyst" theory. According to this theory, the papyri are exactly what professional Egyptologists say they are. But, despite Joseph Smith's belief that they contained the writings of Abraham "by his own hand", and despite his telling people he "translated" them, he did not really mean "translate". He meant that he "received revelation about something true". In other words, the papyri served as a means, a catalyst, by which God sent revelation into Joseph's mind about true events and doctrines involving Abraham, even though the papyri had nothing to do with Abraham.

Whatever else someone might make of that theory, it was not what I had been taught. And to be frank, it seemed to strain credibility, especially in the context of Joseph Smith's other claims about translations. The *Book of Mormon* and the *Book of Abraham* are prime examples, but there are others too. Along with the *Book of Abraham* were more scrolls that Joseph brashly identified as containing the writings of Joseph of Egypt. Well, those papyri were with the others discovered in 1967, and they have nothing to do with Joseph of Egypt.

Another incident concerned the Kinderhook Plates, a set of six brass plates "discovered" by a group of men

---

[28] Palmer, *Mormon Origins*, 21–24.

near Kinderhook, Illinois. Someone brought the plates to Joseph Smith in April of 1843, and as recorded by Joseph Smith's clerk William Clayton, Joseph declared that he had "translated a portion and ... they contain the history of a person with whom they were found and he was a descendant of Ham through the loins of Pharaoh king of Egypt."[29] Parley P. Pratt also wrote about Joseph's translation of those plates. Joseph is reported to have used the Egyptian alphabet and grammar documents noted above in his decipherment of the contents of the Kinderhook Plates.[30] The church touted this discovery at the time in its newspaper, *Times and Seasons*.[31] The plates were later shown to be a hoax perpetrated by the men who "found" them and brought them to Joseph Smith.

In 1842, a Protestant minister is reported to have come to Joseph Smith bearing a well-known Greek psalter (that is, a copy of the Psalms in Greek). He asked Joseph to tell him what they were, and Joseph declared the manuscript was not Greek, but a "dictionary of Egyptian hieroglyphics". He said the capital letters at the beginning of each sentence were Egyptian, and the letters that followed were "the interpretation of the hieroglyphics, written in the reformed Egyptian", like the characters "on the golden plates".[32] When confronted about the incident by the Protestant minister, Joseph's close associate Willard Richards said that sometimes Joseph "speaks as a prophet,

[29] Palmer, *Mormon Origins*, 31.

[30] "Grammar and Alphabet of the Egyptian Language, circa July–circa November 1835", Joseph Smith Papers, Church History Library of the Church of Jesus Christ of Latter-day Saints in Salt Lake City, Utah, https://www.josephsmithpapers.org/paper-summary/grammar-and-alphabet-of-the-egyptian-language-circa-july-circa-november-1835/1.

[31] "Ancient Records", *Times and Seasons*, May 1, 1843, https://contentdm.lib.byu.edu/digital/collection/NCMP1820-1846/id/8507.

[32] Palmer, *Mormon Origins*, 34–35.

and sometimes as a mere man",[33] a helpful escape hatch. Joseph himself would later adopt a modified version of this mantra: "a prophet [is] a prophet only when he [is] acting as such"[34]—a refrain church leaders repeat to this day.

It is difficult as a faithful Mormon to remove one's blinders on these topics and assess them in a straightforward and honest way. I thought to myself at the time, if the claim "Joseph Smith had a gift from God to translate ancient languages" were presented to anyone outside the church who was disinterested in the answer, I seriously doubt a single reasonable person would believe anything other than that either Joseph Smith was committing fraud or he was delusional. Joseph had no gift when it came to translating ancient documents.

Contradictory Theology and Historical Revisionism

Another serious difficulty for me came in learning about how the church's theology had changed radically over time, in contradictory ways, and how the church seems to have worked throughout its history to obscure those changes through historical backdating or revision. I was left with a distinct sense that the religion I belonged to bore little resemblance to the one for which some of my ancestors had crossed the plains. It seemed less correct to speak of *the* Church of Jesus Christ of Latter-day Saints than it did to speak of the *Churches* of Jesus Christ of Latter-day Saints.

The earliest documents in Mormonism evince beliefs in God that are trinitarian-like. I say trinitarian-*like* because

[33] Palmer, *Mormon Origins*, 34–35.
[34] Smith, *History*, 5:265.

most of the ideas are not theologically correct from a trinitarian point of view. More specifically, early Mormonism
abounds with what is called "modalism", the idea that God
the Father and Jesus Christ are numerically identical but
represent different "modes" of the one true God.

The *Book of Mormon*'s original 1830 text expresses
modalistic theology. Indeed, at times it seems that modalism is one of the overarching and self-conscious aims
of the book. The vision given to Nephi in 1 Nephi 11
explains the birth of Jesus as "the condescension *of God*",[35]
calling Mary, "the mother *of God*"—which is actually
an orthodox trinitarian formula if "God" is used to mean
God the Son. However, the angel says to Nephi at the
end of the vision, "Behold the Lamb of God, yea, *even the
Eternal Father.*" This is not traditional incarnation theology. Rather, in the *Book of Mormon*, the person of Jesus
is the "Son of God" *because he is God*, numerically, and
"Son" indicates the *mode* he is in—the Spirit come down
in the flesh.

Some such verses were edited in later editions of the
Book of Mormon. But the imprints of modalism still abound.
A passage in 2 Nephi 11:7 argues the numerical identity
of the Person of Christ with the Father, stating that "if
there be no Christ there be no God; and if there be no
God we are not, for there could have been no creation.
But there is a God, and he is Christ." The entire argument is one for the numerical identity of the Father and
the Son.

The dialogue in Alma chapter 11 between Amulek and
Zeezrom is also geared toward modalism. Zeezrom asks,
"Is there more than one God?" to which Amulek answers,
"No." Zeezrom then asks, "Who is he that shall come? Is

---

[35] All emphasis in quotations from the *Book of Mormon* is mine.

it the Son of God?" and Amulek answers, "Yea." Zeez-
rom finishes, "Is the Son of God the very Eternal Father?
And Amulek said unto him: Yea, he is the very Eternal
Father."

Mosiah 15 probably contains the clearest modalism in
the *Book of Mormon*:

> I would that ye should understand that God himself shall
> come down among the children of men, and shall redeem
> his people. And because he dwelleth in the flesh he shall
> be called the Son of God, and having subjected the flesh
> to the will of the Father, being the Father and the Son—
> the Father, because he was conceived by the power of
> God; and the Son, because of the flesh; thus becoming the
> Father and the Son—and they are one God, yea the very
> Eternal Father of heaven and of Earth. And thus the flesh
> becoming subject to the Spirit, or the Son to the Father,
> being one God, suffered temptation, and yieldeth not to
> the temptation, but suffereth himself to be mocked, and
> scourged, and cast out, and disowned by his people.

This chapter was a perennial head-scratcher for me even
in my most faithful days. But when viewed through the
lens of modalism, it becomes clear.

Mormon responses to the charge that the *Book of Mormon* teaches modalism often consist of pointing to verses
that could be read to suggest something other than modalism, including the visit of the resurrected Jesus to the
Nephites in 3 Nephi. But actually, that chapter, on its own
and when read with another chapter later in the book,
confirms the modalism of the *Book of Mormon*.

In 3 Nephi, just following a cataclysmic earthquake and
darkness, the people gather at the temple and are discussing these great events. They hear a voice from heaven
announce, "Behold my Beloved Son, in whom I am well

pleased, in whom I have glorified my name—hear ye him." They then see Jesus descend from heaven, and Jesus announces unequivocally, "I am the God of Israel, and the God of the whole earth." Jesus repeats multiple times "the Father and I are one" during his visit.

At first blush, this may appear simply trinitarian, rather than modalistic. But later in the book of Ether—a book that comes long before the visit in 3 Nephi chronologically but that is placed after it in the *Book of Mormon*—the prophet known as the Brother of Jared is preparing to set out on an ocean voyage and needs a way to light the barges his people will travel in. He ultimately prays to "the Lord" to touch some stones so that they will glow white and give them light on the journey. "The Lord" does so, first revealing his "finger", which the Brother of Jared comments "was as the finger of a man, like unto flesh and blood". "The Lord" then reveals his whole spiritual body to the Brother of Jared and also tells him, "I am he who was prepared from the foundation of the world to redeem my people. Behold, I am Jesus Christ. *I am the Father and the Son.*" He further explains, "This body, which ye now behold, is the body of my spirit; and man have I created after the body of my spirit; and even as I appear unto thee to be in the spirit will I appear unto my people in the flesh." The supposed *Book of Mormon* redactor Moroni then interjects into the account in Ether, "Jesus showed himself unto this man in the spirit, even after the manner and in the likeness of the same body even as he showed himself unto the Nephites. And he ministered unto [the Brother of Jared] even as he ministered unto the Nephites; *and all this, that this many might know that he was God.*" Thus, the narrative explicitly connects Jesus' visit in 3 Nephi to the modalist teaching of Ether (and, with the phrase "I am the Father and the

Son" to other modalistic teachings contained throughout the *Book of Mormon*).

In 1837, Joseph Smith and Oliver Cowdery revised the text of the *Book of Mormon*. They mainly made grammatical changes but also conspicuously altered certain passages in ways that seemed to put a greater emphasis on the distinction between God the Father and Jesus Christ. Mary was no longer the "mother of God" but "the Mother of the Son of God". Nor did the book read, "Behold the Lamb of God, yea, even the Eternal Father" but "yea, even the Son of the Eternal Father". They didn't change every verse espousing modalism, but these changes are significant in light of the changes in Mormon theology since the *Book of Mormon*'s publication in 1830.

By the mid-1830s, Joseph Smith's beliefs about God the Father and Jesus Christ had changed. At that time, the Fifth Lecture in a book called *Lectures on Faith* presents the beliefs of Mormon leaders (including Joseph Smith and Sidney Rigdon) about "the Godhead—the Father, Son, and Holy Spirit". The lecture is quite unmistakable in its theology: "How many personages are there in the Godhead? Two: the Father and the Son." The Father is described as "a personage of *spirit*", whereas the Son is "a personage *of tabernacle*". The two are described in a different sense from the earlier teachings of the *Book of Mormon*. And Jesus is presented as being flesh, *in contrast* to the Father, who is spirit. Moreover, according to this teaching, "the Father and the Son possess the same mind", and the answer to the question "What is that mind?" is given as "the Holy Spirit". The Holy Spirit is not a personal being but the shared mind of the Father and the Son. This "foregoing account of the Godhead" is said to present "a sure foundation for the exercise of faith … unto life and salvation".[36] Such teaching necessitated some revision of the *Book of Mormon* to blur the book's theology so that it could be said to conform to later beliefs.

This retroactive change was particularly necessary because the *Lectures* were not unofficial theological speculation. They were official doctrine of the church, approved in the formal solemn manner required for canonical stature. In 1835, Joseph Smith, Sidney Rigdon, Oliver Cowdery, and Frederick Williams compiled the *Lectures on Faith* together with a selection of revelations previously given to Joseph Smith, some of which had been published in the earlier book, *The Book of Commandments*, and entitled the new compilation *Doctrine and Covenants*.

As explained in the official introduction to the first edition, an introduction signed by the four men above, "The first part of the book" contains "a series of lectures" and was included "in consequence of their embracing *important doctrine of salvation*.... The second part contains items or principles for the regulation of the Church as taken from the revelations" given to Joseph Smith.[37] That is to say, the "doctrine" of the book was contained in the *Lectures on Faith*. The "covenants" were contained in the subsequent sections of revelations.

The book was presented to the "general assembly of the Church" so as to be approved as "a rule of faith and practice to the Church".[38] In the assembly, "President Cowdery arose and introduced the 'Book of Doctrine and Covenants'.... W.W. Phelps bore record that the book presented to the assembly was true. President

[36] N.B. Lundwall, ed., *A Compilation Containing the Lectures on Faith* (Salt Lake City: Bookcraft Inc., [1940]), lecture 5 (emphasis mine).

[37] Smith, *History*, 2:243 (emphasis mine).

[38] Smith, *History*, 2:243.

John Whitmer, also, rose and testified that it was true."
After more testimony, each of the relevant councils and
quorums of the church accepted and acknowledged them
"as the doctrine and covenants of their faith by a unani-
mous vote".[39]

But the journey was not over. By the Nauvoo period,
Joseph had received a revelation on April 2, 1843, that
"the Father has a body of *flesh and bones as tangible as man's*;
the Son also; but the Holy Ghost has not a body of flesh
and bones, *but is a personage of Spirit*."[40] This presented yet
another contradiction and another problem. The Father,
according to the *Lectures on Faith*, was a personage of spirit,
while the Son was a personage of flesh. And the Holy
Ghost was *not* a personage at all, but the shared mind of
the Father and the Son. This revelation was not officially
added to Mormon Scripture until 1876, during the Presidency of Brigham Young in Utah, and coexisted quite
uncomfortably with the *Lectures on Faith* for forty-five
years until, in the wake of yet another significant theological revision, the *Lectures on Faith* were unceremoniously
removed entirely from *Doctrine and Covenants* in 1921.

The church provided the following curt explanation:
" 'Lectures on Faith,' which were bound in with the *Doctrine and Covenants* in some of its former issues, are not
included in this edition. Those lessons were ... never presented to nor accepted by the Church as being otherwise
than theological lectures or lessons."[41] It is hard to square
this with the historical record, which shows they were officially canonized and were taken as a sure rule of faith on

[39] Smith, *History*, 2:244.

[40] *Doctrine and Covenants* 98:22 (emphasis mine).

[41] Introduction to *Doctrine and Covenants of the Church of Jesus Christ of Latter-
day Saints* (Salt Lake City: Church of Jesus Christ of Latter-day Saints, 1921), v.

which salvation was based, but the disavowal was necessary if the church was going to change its theology and maintain some appearance of consistency. While not as forceful as an 1844 speech given by Joseph Smith when people questioned his new teaching on the plurality of gods, the effect of the church's decision to remove the *Lectures on Faith* and say they were never doctrine struck me as similar to Joseph's assurance to his audience, "I have always and in all congregations when I have preached [on the subject of the Deity,] it has been the plurality of Gods. It has been preached for 15 years. I have always declared God to be a distinct personage, Jesus Christ a separate and distinct personage from God the Father, and the Holy Ghost was a distinct personage and a Spirit: and these three constitute three distinct personages and three Gods."[42]

I saw a pattern emerging in this and other issues. For instance, I was rather alarmed to learn that in the early years of the church, there was no hierarchal concept of the "priesthood" and priesthood offices as would later develop around 1834 and 1835, a time when Joseph Smith was facing a crisis of authority for a number of reasons. Indeed, those impressive appearances of John the Baptist, restoring the Aaronic priesthood to Joseph Smith and Oliver Cowdery in May 1829, and the later visit from Peter, James, and John, who restored the Melchizedek priesthood to them, do not appear in the historical record until 1834, when Oliver Cowdery first began suggesting angelic visitors had given them their authority in this manner.

Early church leaders David Whitmer and William McLellin both said that they had never heard any such

---

[42] Ronald E. Bartholomew, "The Textual Development of D&C 130:22 and the Embodiment of the Holy Ghost", *BYU Studies Quarterly* 52, no. 3 (2013): 7.

story until the mid-1830s, and neither believed those events occurred. These events were retroactively added into *preexisting* revelations that had been printed in the earlier *Book of Commandments* when the 1835 *Doctrine and Covenants* was published. The lack of any contemporaneous evidence of the appearances and the later revisions to revelations dated years earlier led even faithful Mormon historian Richard Bushman to admit, "The late appearance of these accounts raises the possibility of later fabrication."[43]

The very identity of God the Father appeared to me to be unstable. Expounding Joseph Smith's teachings on the plurality of gods, polygamy, and the Temple Endowment as then taught, Brigham Young taught the Mormons of his time that Earth was the testing ground for the spirit children of a particular man who had reached godhood, Adam, who took one of his wives, Eve, and came to Earth and fell so that they could provide mortal bodies for their spirit children—us! In other words, he taught the explicit mechanics of the Mormon doctrine of "exaltation". He thundered from the pulpit, "Now hear it, O inhabitants of the earth, Jew and Gentile, Saint and sinner!... [Adam] is our FATHER and our GOD, and the only God with whom WE have to do."[44] This Adam then appeared at the meridian of time and *physically begot* Jesus Christ with "the Virgin Mary"[45] just "as we were of our fathers"[46]— that is, through sexual intercourse. The doctrine was controversial but gained significant prominence, becoming part of numerous discourses by high-ranking church leaders and being sung in hymns, for example:

[43] Richard Bushman, *Joseph Smith: Rough Stone Rolling* (New York: Alfred A. Knopf, 2005), 15.

[44] Brigham Young, *The Journal of Discourses* (London, 1854), 1:51.

[45] Young, *Discourses*, 1:51.

[46] Young, *Discourses*, 8:115; see also 1:238 and 4:218.

We believe in our God, the Prince of his race,
The archangel Michael, the Ancient of Days
Our own Father Adam, earth's Lord as is plain,
Who'll counsel and fight for His children again.[47]

The doctrine was even taught in the Temple Endowment ceremony for decades following Brigham Young's introduction of it in 1877 to the part of the ceremony known as the "lecture at the veil".

But the "Adam-God" doctrine did not sit well with many people, including some subsequent church leaders. So it had to go. At first, it would be sidelined as a mystery not to be dug too deeply into;[48] then later its status as an *official* church teaching was denied;[49] ultimately, it was explicitly condemned as heretical, with some church leaders denying or obscuring the fact that it was ever taught in the first place, given the awkwardness of the conclusion that the prophet of God had taught false doctrines. Church President Spencer W. Kimball stated matter-of-factly in 1976 that "the Adam-God theory" is not "orthodox truth" and pronounced, "We denounce that theory and hope that everyone will be cautioned against this and other kinds of false doctrine."[50] Elder Mark. E. Peterson asked, "Was Adam our God, or did God become Adam?

[47] "We Believe in Our God", in *Sacred Hymns and Spiritual Songs for the Church of Jesus Christ of Latter-day Saints*, 11th ed. (Liverpool: F.D. Richards, 1856).

[48] See, for example, David John Buerger, "The Adam-God Doctrine", *Dialogue: A Journal of Mormon Thought* 15, no. 1 (1982): 14–58.

[49] See, for example, B.H Roberts, "Answer Given to 'Ten Reasons Why "Christians" Can Not Fellowship with Latter-Day Saints'", *Deseret News*, July 23, 1921 ("As a matter of fact, the 'Mormon' church does not teach that doctrine.").

[50] Spencer W. Kimball, "Our Own Liahona" (146th Semiannual General Conference, Salt Lake City, Priesthood Session, October 2, 1976), https://www.churchofjesuschrist.org/study/general-conference/1976/10/our-own-liahona?lang=eng.

Ridiculous!"[51] Elder Bruce R. McConkie *privately* admitted in a letter to prominent Mormon Eugene England that "President Young did teach that Adam was the Father of our spirits",[52] but taught *publicly*:

> There are those who believe or say they believe that Adam is our father and our god, that he is the father of our spirits and our bodies, and that he is the one we worship. The devil keeps this heresy alive as a means of obtaining converts to cultism. It is contrary to the whole Plan of Salvation set forth in the scriptures, and anyone who has read the Book of Moses, and anyone who has received the temple endowment, and who yet believes the Adam-God theory does not deserve to be saved.[53]

Such statements, invoking the Temple Endowment and the Mormon Scriptures, were somewhat disingenuous in light of the fact that the identities of the various characters in the Endowment drama—Elohim, Jehovah, and Michael (Adam)—were not even defined in the way they are now until the early twentieth century.[54] Reading about these matters gave me a bigger picture of my faith and left me with the disorienting sense that I did not even understand what my religion really was or had ever been. It seemed as if almost nothing was as it appeared.

---

[51] Elder Mark E. Petersen, "Adam, the Archangel" (150th Semiannual Conference of the Church of Jesus Christ of Latter-day Saints, Salt Lake City, October 4, 1980), *Ensign*, November 1980, https://www.churchofjesuschrist.org/study/ensign/1980/11/adam-the-archangel?lang=eng.

[52] Letter from Elder Bruce R. McConkie to Eugene England (February 19, 1981).

[53] Bruce R. McConkie, "The Seven Deadly Heresies" (fireside address, Brigham Young University, June 1, 1980), https://speeches.byu.edu/talks/bruce-r-mcconkie_seven-deadly-heresies/. The written version of the speech replaces "does not deserve to be saved" with "has no excuse whatever for being led astray by [it]".

[54] See Boyd Kirkland, "Jehovah as the Father: The Development of the Mormon Jehovah Doctrine", *Sunstone* 9, no. 2 (1984): 36–44.

Polygamy and Polyandry

I had always known that Joseph Smith had practiced polygamy, but I did not know the details, which is where, they
say, the Devil is. And that was certainly true in this case.

When Joseph began having relationships with women
other than his wife Emma is debatable. There is some
evidence that the famous and tear-jerking story I mentioned earlier of Joseph Smith being ripped from his bed
in the middle of the night and tarred and feathered, was
less an incident of religious persecution and more indicative of the chickens of Joseph's sexual escapades coming home to roost. On the night of the event, March
24, 1832, Joseph had been then staying in the home of
John and Alice Johnson for some time. Among the couple's many children was fifteen-year-old Marinda Nancy.
According to Luke Johnson, Marinda's brother, one of
the principal objects of the mob of some fifty people who
attacked Joseph that night was to castrate him. Luke Johnson reported that they tore off Joseph's underclothing and
stretched him out on a board. A "Dr. Dennison" had been
brought along to perform the castration, but the doctor's
"heart failed him" when he "saw the prophet stripped and
stretched on the plank".[55]

Scholars do not appear to dispute that there was a doctor
brought to the scene for the purpose of castrating Joseph
Smith.[56] But the reason for this usually omitted detail of
the otherwise compassion-inducing story is that the motivation of the mob is debated and subject to some unclear
evidence. One (late) account is that the mob included one
of Marinda Nancy's brothers, and the planned castration

---

[55] Todd Compton, *In Sacred Loneliness: The Plural Wives of Joseph Smith* (Salt
Lake City: Signature Books, 1997), 231.

[56] Compare Compton, *Sacred Loneliness*, 231, with Bushman, *Joseph Smith:
Rough Stone Rolling*, 179.

was because Joseph had become too familiar with her. Marinda Nancy later became one of Joseph Smith's plural wives. Some historians argue that since Joseph Smith first received a revelation on polygamy while he was working on his "translation" of the Bible in 1831, a project he carried out from the Johnson home, he may have begun experimenting with extramarital affairs at this point, resulting in his close shave with frontier justice.

Mormon scholar Todd Compton plausibly concludes that the late account has some indicia of unreliability and that there is no conclusive evidence that Marinda Nancy became Joseph's first plural wife *at that time* (rather than later, which Compton agrees she did). My own read of the history would be a bit less favorable to Joseph with regard to that incident, because whether or not he had a sexual relationship with Marinda Nancy at that time, *no one could be shocked if he had,* as it fits a fairly clear pattern of behavior for Joseph Smith. It is consistent with the character and actions of the man during a significant stretch of his life that began if not then, only a very short time later.

Moreover, as with so many other aspects of Mormonism, events in Joseph's life that occurred in one context are frequently seen to take on a new context later on. Magical treasure quests are recast as a religious calling from an angel, and there is something of the same flavor with regard to Joseph's sexual exploits. According to Compton, the first undisputed case of Joseph's dalliances with a woman other than Emma—seventeen-year-old Fanny Alger—occurred in 1833 while Joseph had the young woman boarding in his home. For some scholars like Compton, this is "perhaps the first plural marriage in Mormon history",[57] but Compton is forced to admit that "the earliest contemporary reference to the Smith-Alger relationship"—a letter by Oliver

---

[57] Compton, *Sacred Loneliness*, 26.

Cowdery—presents no marriage but, to quote Cowdery at the time, "a dirty, nasty, filthy affair".[58] Compton's sources for arguing that "nineteenth century Mormons ... regarded the Smith-Alger relation as a marriage" are, as he acknowledges, from a much later time during the heyday of polygamy, and he acknowledges that other scholars view many of those statements calling it a "sealing" or "marriage" as "superimpos[ing] a later understanding of polygamy onto a sexual liaison."[59]

The view of those scholars struck me as much more persuasive, because, as noted above, this teaching, too, seemed to fit a pattern similar to that of a number of other church teachings: past events, sometimes very uncomfortable ones, are recast in a new light and treated as if they had occurred within the context of the new theology rather than in the context in which they actually happened. As most Mormons reading all of these dates will immediately intuit, there is a *big* theological problem with Joseph Smith's purporting to be sealed to a plural wife before April 3, 1836: the church claims that Joseph did not receive the priesthood power to *seal families* until a visitation from Elijah the prophet in the temple of Kirtland, Ohio, that day which, like the supposed visit of John the Baptist and Peter, James, and John, "restored" priesthood powers lost from the Earth during the Great Apostasy. Joseph's relationship with Fanny Alger does not align with the timeline of events on which the church's traditional story depends.

Reasonable minds can disagree about whether the relationship between Joseph Smith and Fanny Alger was a "marriage" or an "affair", and I would simply encourage people to read for themselves and make up their own minds. But at the time I read this information, whether

[58] Compton, *Sacred Loneliness*, 28.
[59] Compton, *Sacred Loneliness*, 28.

Joseph Smith believed he was receiving divine revelations or whether an affair gave rise to a religious doctrine didn't really matter to me. The details were too much and turned my stomach. The same goes for debates over which marriages, precisely, involved sexual relations and which did not. The evidence is simply undeniable, as forthright scholars like Compton agree, that a number of Smith's marriages—unsurprisingly—involved Joseph and his plural wife having sex, including Fanny Alger. Poor Emma Smith had to kick out young women staying in her home whom she discovered to be Joseph's plural wives on several occasions. All told, Joseph Smith married dozens of women, including eleven who were married to other men (a practice called polyandry), ranging from ages fourteen through fifty-six.

Rumors of Joseph Smith's irregular marital arrangements began making the rounds shortly after the Alger incident and, according to Compton, are likely the genesis of a doctrinal "Articles on Marriage" promulgated at that same time in the 1835 *Doctrine and Covenants*, which stated: "Inasmuch as this Church of Christ has been reproached with the crime of fornication, and polygamy, we declare that we believe that one man should have one wife, and one woman but one husband, except in case of death, when either is at liberty to marry again."[60] This scripture stayed on the books through the entirety of Joseph Smith's lifetime, including the Nauvoo period in which polygamy was rampant and Joseph had accumulated dozens of wives. Joseph Smith consistently denied direct accusations

[60] "Doctrine and Covenants, 1835", p. 251, Joseph Smith Papers, Church History Library of the Church of Jesus Christ of Latter-day Saints in Salt Lake City, Utah, https://www.josephsmithpapers.org/paper-summary/doctrine-and-covenants-1835/259.

of polygamy in public on multiple occasions, at times even pointing to the 1835 "Articles on Marriage" as proof of the church's rejection of polygamy. It was simply unbelievable to me to see Joseph Smith declare—at a time when he had some thirty wives—"What thing it is for a man to be accused of committing adultery, and having seven wives, when I can only find one."[61]

Deception and polygamy went hand in hand. I had always been taught that the church stopped practicing polygamy in 1890, when President Wilford Woodruff issued what is called "Manifesto 1". I was taught this countless times. When I was a missionary, during the October 2007 General Conference, Mormon Apostle Russell Ballard reiterated this common Mormon assertion, and I took special note of it in my journal as I took notes on each talk: "Polygamy in 1890 no longer practiced." As he put it, "Polygamy, a limited practice in the early pioneer days of the Church, was discontinued in 1890, some 117 years ago."[62] Yet I learned this was not true. Church leaders, including Wilford Woodruff, who signed the Manifesto, continued to authorize many polygamous marriages for years after the Manifesto, and the church simply prevaricated for more than a decade. It was not until 1904 that the church began to get serious about the issue, and that was because of the public and embarrassing Reed Smoot hearing before Congress, in which Mormon President Joseph F. Smith prevaricated to such an extent that he is reasonably open to a charge of perjury, and the church's

---

[61] Smith, *History*, 6:411.

[62] M. Russell Ballard, "Faith, Family, Fact, and Fruits" (177th Semiannual General Conference of the Church of Jesus Christ of Latter-day Saints, Salt Lake City, Saturday Afternoon Session, October 2007), https://www.church ofjesuschrist.org/study/general-conference/2007/10/faith-family-facts-and -fruits?lang=eng.

efforts did not result in a hard stop to polygamy until the early 1930s.[63]

Perhaps most painful of all for me when I learned the details of polygamy (very few of which are recounted here) was the realization that one of the doctrines of my faith that had meant so much to me—the eternal family, the idea that my wife and I could be sealed together forever—was rooted in Joseph Smith's and his other male contemporaries' sexual liaisons. A doctrine that seems so fundamentally wholesome on its face was in fact based on something fundamentally wrong.

Anti-Intellectualism

Perhaps the last issue really to click for me was the church's antagonism during the twentieth century, and the beginning of the twenty-first, to an intellectually honest approach to difficult issues in its history. I don't want to paint with too broad a brush, but I realized that according to existing accounts, not all church leaders agreed with the approach the church was taking. There were some who seemed more sympathetic at times to a more accurate portrayal of the church's history, but that position did not win out. Rather, the church opted to take a position of suppressing information that was not "faith promoting", discouraging members from researching the church's history other than as retold in officially approved sources, labeling all materials that presented a narrative

[63] See D. Michael Quinn, "LDS Church Authority and New Plural Marriages, 1890–1904", *Dialogue: A Journal of Mormon Thought* 18, no. 1 (Spring 1985): 9–105. See also Cristina Rosetti, "'Hysteria Excommunicatus': Loyalty Oaths, Excommunication, and the Forging of a Mormon Identity", *The Journal of Mormon History* 47, no. 3 (July 2021): 24–27.

that deviated from the official retelling of church history "anti-Mormon", and excommunicating those who became too loud when they discovered the details of the church's founding.

I think nearly all my life, from friends, family, and other people in the church, I had heard of the infamous anti-Mormon, Fawn Brodie. All I knew was that her book about Joseph Smith, *No Man Knows My History*, was not to be read, as it was merely an attack on the church and an attempt to lead people away from the faith, on par with scandal-mongering works like *The God Makers*, an evangelical Protestant film lampooning Mormonism and making, at times, wildly inaccurate and sensational claims about the faith. Mormon Professor Hugh Nibley excoriated Brodie's work in his cleverly titled response, *No Ma'am, That's Not History*[64]—or at least I thought it was clever when I was in my early twenties and did not really understand the difference between attacking people and attacking arguments, and the aims of academic scholarship versus those of polemics.

Although I am embarrassed to admit it, I was caught off guard to learn that Brodie's book was not some pulp sensationalism, but *the seminal scholarly biography* of Joseph Smith. Acclaimed Mormon historian Richard Bushman's 2005 biography—usually considered a more "faithful" biography in the sense that it is an attempt at promoting faith in Joseph Smith—acknowledges in the introduction that Brodie's book was a "landmark".[65] Philosophers are prone to say that all of Western philosophy is merely a footnote to Plato—I

[64] Hugh Nibley, *No Ma'am, That's Not History: A Brief Review of Mrs. Brodie's Reluctant Vindication of a Prophet She Seeks to Expose* (Salt Lake City: Bookcraft, 1969).

[65] Bushman, *Joseph Smith: Rough Stone Rolling*, xxii.

discovered that all of Mormon history is merely a footnote to Brodie. Not all of Brodie's conclusions have stood the test of time, but in the main, her work has held up since its publication in the 1940s and is still likely the definitive work on Joseph Smith. I finished the book while on an airplane and will never forget weeping at the scene of the mob murdering Joseph Smith at Carthage Jail. I cried, not as I had before at the so-called "martyrdom" of a prophet; rather, I felt incredibly sorry for someone I saw, for the first time, as a real person. Unlike the untouchable and heroic Joseph of church hagiography, the book presented a believable, at times compelling, picture of a tragic and complicated man whose equal parts of swindling and sincerity, brashness and bravado, led to his wild success and violent undoing.

Brodie was the niece of future church president, and then apostle, David O. McKay. Her book caused an uproar. She was not really an active participant in the church when she wrote the book, but of course she received a summons in 1946—which many surmise was issued at the behest of her uncle—to appear before her local church authorities in New England. Brodie's book presented Joseph as a charlatan and a sex-fiend—controversial, but not implausible interpretations of history (I myself take a more sympathetic view, more akin to the pious-manipulator theory advanced by historian Dan Vogel). Brodie was to answer charges of "asserting matters as truths which deny the divine origin of the *Book of Mormon*, the restoration of the Priesthood and of Christ's Church through the instrumentality of the Prophet Joseph Smith".[66] She did not show up but was excommunicated nonetheless.

Ironically, however, later church scholars who were attempting to be faithful both to history and to the belief

---

[66] Newell G. Bringhurst, "Fawn Brodie and Her Quest for Independence", *Dialogue: A Journal of Mormon Thought* 22, no. 2 (Summer 1989): 79–95.

in the prophetic calling of Joseph Smith and the truthfulness of the Mormon Church suffered the same fate. The late historian D. Michael Quinn is a tragic example.

Impeccably credentialed, Quinn worked under the famed Leonard Arrington—a revolutionary church historian who, during his brief tenure, tried to push the church's history department in a more honest direction and found himself fired for it—and would produce some of the most important books and articles in Mormon history. Quinn's books were controversial because they presented some facts that simply cannot be reconciled with official church narratives. For example, Quinn believed there is some historical support for a visit from Peter, James, and John, but it came *after* the church was organized on April 6, 1830, and Quinn's developmental treatment of the doctrine of priesthood made people uncomfortable.

Yet Quinn was clearly attempting not to undermine the church, but to help it. When Quinn published an article in 1985 about the polygamy that church leaders had secretly authorized after the 1890 Manifesto, three members of the Quorum of the Twelve Apostles ordered Quinn's stake president to revoke his temple recommendation for "speaking evil of the Lord's anointed".[67] Quinn's article casts little or no judgment on church leaders of that time period and is indeed sympathetic to the predicament they faced.

Later, Quinn became one of the infamous September Six, a cadre of influential Mormon intellectuals excommunicated or disfellowshipped in September 1993 for their controversial writings about church history and theology. Quinn's excommunication ostensibly occurred because he was homosexual (he would not come out for several more

<hr />

[67] D. Michael Quinn, "Background and Fallout of My 1985 Article: 'LDS Church Authority and New Plural Marriages, 1890–1904'", *Sunstone*, January 31, 2020, https://sunstonemagazine.com/background-and-fallout/.

years), but his retelling leaves little room for doubt that apostle Boyd Packer was behind the directive to excommunicate him, and primarily because of his retellings of church history. To his death in early 2021, Quinn believed deeply that the Mormon Church was true.

Boyd Packer was one of many high-ranking church leaders whose views on honest retellings of church history were unequivocal: do not do it. In a 1981 address to Church Education System teachers, he criticized the "temptation for the writer or the teacher of Church history to want to tell everything, whether it is worthy or faith promoting or not". He added, "Some things that are true are not very useful," warning his audience not "to take great pride in publishing something new, particularly if it illustrates a weakness or mistake of a prominent" church figure. "Be careful that you build faith rather than destroy it.... A destroyer of faith—particularly one within the Church, and more particularly one who is employed specifically to build faith—places himself in great spiritual jeopardy." He finished with a clear mission for those who were going to write history about the church if employed by the church: "In the Church we are not neutral. We are one-sided.... We are belligerents defending the good. We are therefore obliged to give preference to and protect all that is represented in the gospel of Jesus Christ, and we have made covenants to do it."[68]

This encapsulates the church's militant attitude toward keeping uncomfortable facts from its members or obscuring historical truths, in order to be faith-promoting, that dominated the church for most of a century.

---

[68] Boyd K. Packer, "The Mantle Is Far, Far Greater Than the Intellect" (address at Brigham Young University, August 22, 1981), https://www.churchofjesus christ.org/study/manual/teaching-seminary-preservice-readings-religion-370 -471-and-475/the-mantle-is-far-far-greater-than-the-intellect?lang=eng.

Church President Joseph Fielding Smith was, earlier in his career, the church's official historian and as such was intimately familiar with the available materials, including the controversial ones that were restricted from most historical research. It is truly astounding that such a person would dedicate an entire section of his influential book *Doctrines of Salvation* to explaining that "seer stones [were] not used in [the] Book of Mormon Translation", insisting that "there is no authentic statement in the history of the Church which states that the use of such a stone was made in the translations."[69]

But that might be unsurprising when you know that this is the same man who, when he came across the earliest version of Joseph Smith's First Vision—which was written in Joseph's own hand in 1832 but unpublished and which did not accord with the later canonized 1838 version—*physically cut it out of the journal* (or ordered a church archivist to do so) and kept it in a private safe in his office for decades. You can see where church history archivists had to Scotch Tape the pages back into the journal if you look at the church's Joseph Smith Papers Project, which now has the account published in high-quality, full-color photos online.[70] The details surrounding the decision to tape the pages back in suggest that intrepid Mormon researchers Jerald and Sandra Tanner had heard of the account and asked Joseph Fielding Smith for access to it, which forced him, in order to avoid embarrassment from the church's "enemies", to put the pages back and provide access to a

[69] Joseph Fielding Smith, *Doctrines of Salvation* (Salt Lake City: Bookcraft, 1956), 3:225.

[70] "History, circa Summer 1832", p. 5, Joseph Smith Papers, Church History Library of the Church of Jesus Christ of Latter-day Saints, Salt Lake City, Utah, https://www.josephsmithpapers.org/paper-summary/history-circa-summer-1832/5.

faithful Mormon researcher at the time so he could produce a transcript of the document.

That effort to undo the damage seems like a striking metaphor, a prefiguring of the church's 2013 essay series. The essays feel forced, clumsy, and transparent—like Scotch Tape trying to mend the torn pages of Joseph Smith's journal. And it did not help that the essays themselves were at times highly misleading.

One of the most egregious is the church's essay on the *Book of Abraham*. Reading that essay, followed by the critique of it (cited in the appendix of this book) by world-renowned Egyptologist Dr. Robert Ritner, will show the reader just how misleading the essay is from the perspective of a competent Egyptologist.

Another prominent example is the church's essay on denying the priesthood to people of African descent. The essay strongly insinuates that it was not "doctrine" but merely "a policy" of the church. And it characterizes explanations for the ban that held sway in the church for over a hundred years as mere "theories" and "opinion of men". But this is all incredibly misleading. As of the writing of this book, the essay leaves conveniently unmentioned and unaddressed one of the most important documents on the matter, the First Presidency's August 17, 1949, official statement (a statement reaffirmed by the church in 1961), that states expressly: "It is not a matter of the declaration of a policy but of direct commandment from the Lord, on which is founded the doctrine of the Church from the days of its organization, to the effect that Negroes may become members of the Church but that they are not entitled to the Priesthood at the present time."[71]

---

[71] Albert Smith, "First Presidency Statement", August 17, 1949, quoted in Lester E. Bush, Jr., "Mormonism's Negro Doctrine: An Historical Overview", *Dialogue: A Journal of Mormon Thought* 34, no. 1 (2001): 46.

The statement continues to quote several "prophets of the Lord" who explained *why* this doctrine exists, including Brigham Young's explanation that people of African descent are "cursed with a skin of blackness" because they are "from the seed of Cain", a curse that would not be removed until "all the rest of the children [of God] have received their blessings in the holy priesthood."[72] Other nonsensical explanations are given as well, including that all black people accepted this curse in the premortal life, because gaining a body was so important, that "no matter what the handicap may be as to the *kind* of bodies they [would] secure", they freely chose to come.[73]

The church rightly disavowed such abhorrent explanations in the 2013 essay, but to suggest to its membership that this teaching and practice was merely a policy (something that can be changed) and not doctrine (something eternally true) is misleading.

Through my studies it was apparent to me that *doctrine*, which the church taught was unchangeable, was in fact changeable to the point that what was doctrine today as taught by a president of the church could easily, a few decades down the line, be condemned as heresy. I felt a complete inability to trust Mormon leadership on the divisive social questions of our time, because the leadership insisted its teachings were based on its "doctrine", yet I was left doubting. Would such beliefs simply be declared to have only been a "policy" in twenty, thirty, or fifty years when it became too socially unacceptable to hold them? What was I supposed to believe?

---

[72] Smith, "First Presidency Statement", quoted in Bush, "Mormonism's Negro Doctrine", 90.

[73] Smith, "First Presidency Statement", quoted in *The Mormon Church and Blacks: A Documentary History*, ed. Matthew L. Harris and Newell G. Bringhurst (Urbana-Champaign, IL: University of Illinois Press, 2015), 66.

The church's perennial emphasis on our feelings, rather than our intellects, began to make dreadful sense to me. If we connect the truthfulness of some abstract proposition— say, Joseph Smith is a prophet of God—to an emotion or feeling we have, it takes on an unfalsifiable quality. Indeed, church leaders want it to be so, as Dallin Oaks taught: "Anyone can disagree with our personal testimony, but no one can refute it."[74] When those emotive experiences stack up over time, along with a lifetime built around the church and the thick community it provides, they become powerful sources of motivated reasoning, leading us to *want desperately* to believe something enough that we will turn down the power of our intellect in order to do so. Negative emotions have a place in the church's teaching as well; they are the "stupor of thought" supposedly indicating to us that something is bad or not true. So when we experience cognitive dissonance—the negative feeling associated with reading or hearing views that contradict our own deeply held views—the church provides us with a framework for rejecting that negative information as spiritually dangerous. God is *warning* us not to read that book about Joseph Smith or not to visit that "anti-Mormon" website.

In a moment of clarity, although it was painful and discomforting, I realized that my feelings had led me terribly astray. They were no more a reliable measure of objective truth about Joseph Smith and the Mormon Church than they were about whether I would get an A on an exam. "The heart is deceitful above all things, and desperately corrupt; who can understand it?" (Jer 17:9).

---

[74] Dallin H. Oaks, "Testimony", *Ensign*, May 2008, https://www.churchof jesuschrist.org/study/ensign/2008/05/testimony?lang=eng.

7

From the Susquehanna to the Tiber

I NOTED IN MY JOURNAL in mid-October 2015 that it was over: "It is hard to put it on paper. But I no longer believe in the Church. I believe in God and His Son, Jesus Christ. And I believe the Church has and will continue to bring me closer to Them. But the truth claims of the Church are without merit. I am not 'leaving' the Church. Carly and I will raise our children in the Church. I just can't go on believing. If I am to have integrity, I have to come clean."

And I did, telling my wife, and later, friends and family. I wrote in communications to loved ones at the time:

> I no longer believe the Church is what it claims to be. I am as sad as you are about this, trust me. I have felt this way for some time. It has been a slowly brooding reality for a couple of years.... This has been the hardest thing that I have ever faced. I have wrung my hands to the bone about telling you. I have written probably 15 draft emails. I have hemmed and hawed. I know that people's reaction to this will be that I never had a testimony, or that I just wanted to sin, or all of the other silly things people use to side-step the real issue: there are legitimate problems with the Church's history and doctrine that the Church has only recently begun to feel the need to address. It is, for many people, myself included, too little, too late....

> Take your time before responding.... I know you are
> disappointed in me. I know that everyone I know, and
> that everyone with whom I have had a relationship in the
> Church for years and years will be disappointed in me.

Those were, at times, painful discussions that were
charged with emotion and caused me and others to say
things we have since regretted. But the responses that
urged me to reconsider only confirmed to me that I had
made the right decision: "You cannot argue the truth of
the Gospel of Jesus Christ. You cannot prove it is true
and you cannot prove it is not true." I had given in to
"the philosophies of men" (an allusion to the doctrines
taught by Satan, as presented in the Temple Endowment),
and the answer was to pray more and have faith and hold
fast to my testimony. Ironically, so many members of the
church with sincere intention do not realize that when
they are confronted with a family member who has doubts
or who has decided the church is not true because of these
historical issues, and their response is to bear testimony—
"But I *know*, beyond a shadow of a doubt, by the power of
the Holy Ghost, that the church is *true!*"—they are giving
precisely the wrong response.

For people who have begun that journey out of Mormonism, the only thing that will likely stop it is a rational
response to their legitimate questions and an acknowl-
edgement that their questions are legitimate. Invoking a
testimony is the wrong way to respond. The reason is simple: we who have left the church for these reasons tend
to view our testimony as having been built on an illusory
foundation. The sensation of a testimony, at least in my
judgment, would never be felt in the first place if listeners
knew the full account of Mormon history beforehand. It
is only the sanitized version that has the compelling story

behind it to move people emotionally into "knowing" the church is true. To be sure, many people find a way to accommodate their testimony after coming to hold heterodox beliefs about the church in light of historical realities, but that is an accommodation, a reaction, which is different from how things would be on a clean slate.

The next couple of years I spent living in a precarious limbo. Having one's faith and entire worldview—moral and religious—wiped away is challenging psychologically, mentally, emotionally, and spiritually. The ever-present sense of loneliness and isolation is impossible to escape. It was made all the more difficult by my commitment not to discuss the details of it with my wife; from 2015 to 2020, we spoke of it only infrequently. I continued to attend church every week with my wife to help her with the children. And we had agreed she would continue to raise the children Mormon, as her faith was still intact. Whatever ward we found ourselves in, I would quietly speak with the bishop and tell him my situation. The bishops were uniformly kind and generous about it, and I volunteered to continue to serve in callings as long as there was no religious teaching or testifying component, which bishops were always glad to hear. When friends or my wife inquired about whether I was thinking of joining another church, my honest answer was no.

I accepted my position in life for what it was and my heritage for what it was. Whether I believed it or not, in some indescribable way, I was still Mormon. It didn't just wash off. So I spent much of my time thinking through Mormonism, trying to see if I, too, like others I was beginning to learn about, could continue on my own religious path within the framework of Mormonism but without holding to the traditional beliefs that I found to be without a sound foundation.

I only wrote in my journal twice more after that fateful October day in 2015: once in November, noting that "my relationship with the Church is complicated and will continue to be so", and then not again until September 25, 2016, when I wrote my last journal entry: "I have dived into heterodoxy/praxis. I have immersed myself in the study of Mormon history. I'm continuing to develop what it is that I believe. But with the current bounds of orthodoxy, I do not fit and cannot claim to have a testimony.... We have since moved to [Virginia], I start work tomorrow, and I've sort of 'come out' re[garding] the Church out here. I feel so much better."

That is the last entry in my journals, which spanned more than eleven years of my life. Recreating the portion of my life that followed, while much closer to the present and thus more readily accessible by memory, is more difficult, although there are some important sources that helped me see how my thinking developed and how it is that I stumbled into Catholicism (and I do believe "stumbled" is the right word here), including my internet search history and online book-purchase records.

I was exploring what a sort of "reformed" Mormonism might look like and what kinds of beliefs it might accommodate. For instance, perhaps like some forward-thinking Mormons I knew, I could merely accept the *Book of Mormon* as pseudepigraphal work, but Scripture nonetheless. A number of Mormon writers have made comparisons between how certain books of the Old and New Testament with likely different authorial origin than has long been ascribed to them could provide a model for Mormon scripture in which the *Book of Mormon* could comfortably reside. There was no Lehi, no Nephi, in *reality*, as there may have been no historical Job, but chasing such hyperliteralism may be missing the point of the inspired author in the first place. Or so the thinking would go.

The role of the prophet might also be seen as quite different in this framework. Perhaps prophets are in some sense special examples in their connection to God and their drive to understand the divine will for mankind. But in light of the Mormon history of prophets, it was clear that they, too, could err, even when it came to matters of faith that they claimed were of divine origin. Such reconfigurations of the traditional concept of Mormon prophets would be necessary to account for moral blunders in what had been prophetically pronounced teachings, such as Adam-God, polygamy, and the racial priesthood ban.

This framework might reinterpret Mormonism's early key events in important ways. For instance, perhaps the concept of the priesthood on which Joseph Smith ultimately settled was correct, but that concept was one that was gradually revealed to him in a much less dramatic way than Mormons traditionally believed. Similarly, perhaps the revelation on polygamy had a kernel that ultimately wound up being eternally true: the truth that families could be sealed together forever. The argument would posit that this concept came gradually to Joseph as he clearly stumbled, at times very hard, and missed the mark of God's revelation by viewing it in polygamist terms in those early years, which took time to correct. In this way, it was less like the prophets were likely to be trustworthy about *specific* revelatory acts—such as the polygamy revelation itself or the purported revelation to Wilford Woodruff to "stop" polygamy in 1890—and more like the idea that in imperceptible and mysterious ways, God guided his church ultimately to land on the correct outcomes, sometimes through the use of actors outside the church hierarchy or even outside the church altogether.

This idea seemed attractive to me on some level, but implausible because of what I perceived as serious difficulties it left in its wake. For example, it was too difficult for me to square this more subtle view of revelation with what I understood to be well-documented fabrications, like the visits of John the Baptist and Peter, James, and John, or the numerous other retroactive changes made to the *Doctrine and Covenants* on a host of other issues. And this smooth developmental theory was also too hard for me to reconcile with much more plausible explanations for, as another example, the obvious and ever-increasing embellishment involved in Joseph Smith's numerous different accounts of his First Vision. It was not that I found my own answer more plausible because of the supernatural elements of Joseph's claims—I never stopped believing in the supernatural—it was that the evidence just seemed overwhelmingly one-sided in the simpler explanations available for Joseph's actions and teachings.

At the end of the day, although I thought much about this idea over the course of a year or so, I always ended up at the same place: the origins of Mormonism seemed to me to be drenched in fabrication and deception, and in ways that were theologically significant. I never expected Joseph Smith to be perfect or something other than a product of his time, which would be unreasonable, but his theological claims were inextricably intertwined with behavior that was highly questionable to me. There was no divorcing Joseph's (to my mind) fraudulent treasure quests from the *Book of Mormon* itself and Joseph's claim to be called as a prophet. The doctrine of eternal families was similarly too attached to polygamy and polyandry, practices whose questionable origins and morality, on their own terms, caused even the most dutiful Mormons I knew to shift uncomfortably in their seats when contemplating what it must actually have been like to agree to Joseph's requests.

These conclusions, however, took time to work out. Toward the end of 2017, influenced by the similar list of the late church historian Leonard Arrington (contained in Greg Prince's wonderful biography of him), I penned a document I called "Proposed Reforms of a Conservative, Lapsed Mormon" that included "establish[ing] a quorum of seventies whose role is theological development", "abolish[ing] the [church's] correlation committee", "permit[ting] non-historical interpretation of the Book of Mormon", "decanoniz[ing]" the *Book of Abraham* and *Doctrine and Covenants* 132 (on polygamy), making the Word of Wisdom "voluntary", "permit[ting] Trinitarian belief" and "the use of the cross", "promulgat[ing] Official Declaration 3, denouncing racism of the early church doctrine and practice", and permitting "members to pay 10% of income for tithing, but permit[ing] it to be designated to humanitarian relief". As any Mormon reading this will likely recognize, those were heady times for me.

My thinking about this evolutionary model was influenced by my legal training and thinking about how the Common Law of England worked. For centuries, legal rules were promulgated as the result of specific adjudications of specific disputes between parties. And that "common law" evolved over time in response to varying changes in social circumstance. Working from this paradigm, I got around 3,400 words into a to-this-day-unfinished essay entitled "Enlarge the Place of Thy Tent: Reimagining Mormonism's Theological and Practical Boundaries as Means of Convert Gathering". The essay argued that Mormon theological and practice boundaries should be reimagined in order to be more accepting of a more diverse set of beliefs and practices than it then permitted. I noted that the church in fact already permitted some surprising levels of diversity within the bounds of orthodox Mormonism on a number of issues of practice and belief, including the Word of Wisdom, Sabbath Day observance, permissible sexual activity between spouses, and beliefs about the specifics of Mormon exaltation in the afterlife. But my intellectual endeavors kept running into a difficulty: How do you *define* Mormon doctrine? By what criteria can you say what is and what is not official Mormon teaching? You cannot devise a framework for changes or shifts in doctrine if you cannot say with any reasonable certainty what doctrine is in the first place.

Answers to this question were elusive. The closest I could find in more modern times was a single General Conference talk by Elder Neil L. Andersen in 2012 asserting that church doctrine is that which is taught simultaneously by *all* the members of the Quorum of the Twelve and First Presidency.[1] But that seemed problematic. Would that mean that at any given point, one would have to scour the teachings of those fifteen men to determine the things they apparently *all* agreed on at the time, and if there were topics taught by one and not another, they weren't doctrine? In any event, ironically, I couldn't find evidence that all fifteen were teaching that point in 2012 at the time of Elder Andersen's talk, so his principle wound up being self-defeating.

The church's "Articles of Faith", too, seemed obviously deficient in the sense that they were not comprehensive, but only covered a few things and excluded some of the most significant beliefs that nearly all Mormons would consider "doctrine".

During this same time, something else was going on in my life that was undoubtedly driving me. I had begun

---

[1] Neil L. Andersen, "Trial of Your Faith" (182nd Semiannual General Conference of the Church of Jesus Christ of Latter-day Saints, Salt Lake City, Saturday Afternoon Session, October 6, 2012), https://www.churchofjesuschrist.org/study/general-conference/2012/10/trial-of-your-faith?lang=eng.

my career as a practicing lawyer at a large law firm and was having significant success in that endeavor. A career in law is busier than the average occupation by default, but I was spending exceptional amounts of time at work, and moreover, I had transformed my work into a central component of my identity—because I had a large hole in it at that point that needed filling.

Unfortunately, that hole persisted and *couldn't* be filled by anything. I found myself not infrequently crying in my bed in the middle of the night, agonizing over what to make of my life. Was God there? What did that even mean anymore? I felt completely adrift, utterly alone in my life, and nothing seemed to fill the gap, no accolade at work, no bonus, no happy outing with the kids, no fine Scotch, and none of my attempts to live my eclectic version of Mormonism. My very foundations had been swept away and I was alone. I remember lying in bed in tears one night, drunk this time. My wife asked what was wrong, and I responded, "I am so alone."

Each time I had to sit in church and hear someone sing "Praise to the Man", nothing short of rage filled my heart. Every time I caught a glimpse of someone talking about the *Book of Mormon* to my children, I had to leave the room because I could barely contain myself. In my spiritual quest, I felt sad that there was not really a place in Mormonism for someone simply to go and be with God outside of structured Sunday worship and temple worship, which was forbidden to those without a temple recommend. I often wondered aloud how nice it would be if Mormonism had its churches *open*, like other denominations, so people could simply enter to pray. Strolling into large Episcopal or Catholic churches in New York or D.C., I found there was someone always there. People were there, in quiet, praying, lighting candles, sometimes crying. I longed for there to be such a place for me in Mormonism, but there was none.

The only consolation I could find was in attending church on Sundays, taking the Sacrament—something that by the church's standards I shouldn't have been doing but that I considered my only and last connection to Jesus. If there was only *one* thing I associated with Christianity as a fundamental, it was that. Indeed, when my wife asked me whether I would join another church or was thinking about it, I usually responded, "No. The only thing that could get me to change my mind is if the bishop were to tell me I can no longer take the Sacrament."

But something was still not right. At some point, I began to ponder a question that I had not pondered for a long time: How can I be forgiven of sin? How does that work for me now? Is it really just a matter of asking God for forgiveness like I'm doing now? There were things in my life that I felt were just not right, but I had nowhere to deal with them. It was painful.

These two paths—my writing projects about Mormon theology and my own sense of longing for something, I knew not what—began to converge on May 12, 2017, at 10:20 P.M., which is when I made two Google searches: "newman apologia" and "can a non catholic go to confession". The second of these references is easy enough to understand. I was simply curious about whether I might go and talk to a clergyman and unburden my soul, because I felt like I had nowhere else to go. I knew Catholics had confession, so it seemed like a reasonable question. Unfortunately, the answer was no, and it only took a few minutes to find.

But that first reference likely needs unpacking for a non-Catholic audience, and to be completely honest, the explanation of how that Google search came to be is still shrouded in mystery to me. I suspect that somewhere in some way, I had heard about (now Saint) John Henry Newman and found whatever I heard to be strange or at least intriguing. A first-rate intellectual who had taught at Oxford, a theologian, and a member of the clergy of the Church of England, Newman converted to Roman Catholicism in his forties in 1845, at great personal and professional cost. He later wrote an autobiography entitled *Apologia Pro Vita Sua*. In all honesty, I can only speculate about why I searched for it in the first place, as my own review of my Google history for months prior to that day does not provide even the slightest clue about how Newman got on my radar. But he did. And he must have intrigued me enough, because the next day, I visited Newman's Wikipedia page and found something that I do recall seeing and immediately viewing as relevant to my project on Mormon theology: a reference to another book he wrote, called *An Essay on the Development of Christian Doctrine*. I read through the introduction to Newman's essay online in which he discusses his framework of development, and I thought it could provide a useful framework for my project, so I bought the book, read the introduction, and shelved it for the time being.

I also searched for other materials related to my project—for instance, various publications that contained Mormon "creeds" of former times, including a book I had not heard of before by John Jacques called *Catechism for Children: Exhibiting the Prominent Doctrines of the Church of Jesus Christ of Latter-day Saints*. I found it curious that my church used to embrace catechisms but no longer did—there was no single place one could go for a systematic exposition of the doctrine of the Mormon Church, despite the fact that this book had been very popular when it was published in the nineteenth century (reportedly over 35,000 copies and at least six languages). But I *did* know of one church that had such a presentation of its teachings today: the Catholic Church. So I purchased a *Catechism* to get a sense of how other faiths went about this, along with a copy of Newman's *Apologia* and a book by the late Stephen Webb (co-authored with Mormon Alonzo Gaskill) called *Catholic and Mormon: A Theological Conversation*. I read the latter and found the comparing and contrasting of the two faiths rather fascinating. Newman's *Apologia* sat unread on my shelf until I was nearly finished with the last chapter of this book and seeking to understand the apparent influence of Newman on my life and thinking.

On May 13, 2017, I also made a Google search, perhaps as a result of reading the introduction to Newman's essay, for "1st century christianity". Something intrigued me on the Wikipedia page entry because I had never heard of such a thing before: a reference to a group of writers called the "Church Fathers" and in particular the following sentence: "The earliest Church Fathers, within two generations of the Twelve apostles of Christ, are usually called Apostolic Fathers for reportedly knowing and studying under the apostles personally."[2] I don't know if the thought had ever crossed my mind that there may have been people so closely connected to the earliest followers of Jesus who also left writings. But I did not do much with it then.

When my books arrived, I began reading Newman's *Essay on Development* and was struck by the book's erudition—I had never read anything by a Mormon leader that came anywhere close to the intellectual sophistication of that book. "Can you *talk* about faith like this?" As naïve as it was, I was taken aback that, apparently,

---

[2] "Christianity in the 1st Century", Wikipedia, last modified March 16, 2022, https://en.wikipedia.org/wiki/Christianity_in_the_1st_century.

more than 140 years ago, Newman had already worked out for his faith such questions as "What is doctrine?" and had set forth a very sophisticated theory about how doctrine develops over time and how to judge between acceptable and unacceptable developments. Moreover, his critiques of some ideas about doctrine were the same ones that I had made of Elder Andersen's attempt to define Mormon doctrine. As Newman recounts, some Anglicans advocated the position of fifth-century writer Vincent of Lerins, "Quod semper, quod ubique, quod ab omnibus"—that is, Christianity is what has been "held always, everywhere, and by all". To my mind, there were some parallels between this position and the one Elder Andersen had tried to articulate in his 2012 talk. Newman makes an objection similar to my own criticism of Andersen's theory, pointing out (quoting another writer) the "general defect" of this notion: "What is meant by being 'taught *always?*' does it mean in every century, or every year, or every month? Does '*every where*' mean in every country, or in every diocese? And does 'the *Consent of the Fathers*' require us to produce the direct testimony of every one of them?"[3] I scribbled in the margins of these passages, "Elder Andersen on *doctrine.*"

My project on Mormon theology eventually stalled, however. Something that lodged in the back of my mind continued to come to the fore, and I found myself thinking, "I wonder what those 'Apostolic Fathers' believed in. I wonder if it would be interesting to sort of survey and see what useful things I might take from them for my own beliefs." I had this quasi-romantic idea in my mind of living out my life within Mormonism, but with my

---

[3] John Henry Newman, *An Essay on the Development of Christian Doctrine* (London: James Toovey, 1845), 9.

own idiosyncratic beliefs. I'd be "that guy" in the back of the room at church. On May 29, 2017, I searched for "philip schaff early church fathers complete pdf" to find a complete edition of all these writings. A short while later, on what amounted to a complete whim and an arguably unwise purchase at the time, on June 20, 2017, I got an email from eBay that I had won, on a $226.50 bid, "nicene ante-nicene post-nicene church fathers schaff doctrine theology", the listing of a widely known (Protestant) thirty-eight-volume series of the Church Fathers. I say it seemed unwise because I was explicitly only interested in volume one, which contained the writings of the Apostolic Fathers, and I thought to myself, "I really do not care what happened to Christianity once the Roman Catholics got their hands on it in the centuries after that." My expectation was that I would find a number of ideas that probably supported a number of Christian denominations' beliefs, and I could pick, cafeteria-style, what sounded like it would best accommodate me while discarding the rest. But that is not what I found.

Each night, for some time, I would come home, finish any additional work I had, and stay up late into the night reading through the earliest non–New Testament documents that existed. I read, without commentaries or outside texts, roughly chronologically, through the works of the early Christian writers: the *Didache*; Saint Clement of Rome's *Epistle to the Corinthians*; the *Epistle to Diognetus*; Saint Polycarp's *Epistle to the Ephesians* and the account of Polycarp's martyrdom; Saint Ignatius of Antioch's letters to the Ephesians, Mangesians, Trallians, Romans, Philadelphians, Smyrnaens, and his friend Saint Polycarp; the *Epistle of Barnabas*; the existent fragments of the writings of Papias; Saint Justin Martyr's first and second *Apologies* as well as his *Dialogue with Trypho the Jew* and the account of Justin's martyrdom; and then Saint Irenaeus of Lyon's *Against Heresies.*

I had a growing suspicion of what was coming as I read Saint Ignatius' letters. I got very worried when I read Saint Justin's *First Apology.* And when I got to book 3, chapters 3 and 4 of Saint Irenaeus' *Against Heresies,* written in A.D. 180, I thought I had a very big problem on my hands—a Catholic-sized problem. As with the issues that intellectually took me out of Mormonism, I could hardly expect to give a full treatment to the issues that intellectually pushed me into Catholicism. But I will address a few here.

I was raised believing that there was perhaps no other Catholic belief more superstitious and plainly indicative of a Great Apostasy than the belief that the bread and wine become Jesus' Body and Blood during the Mass, which Christians then eat and drink. My views were shaped by people like Elder James E. Talmage, who taught in his book *Jesus the Christ* that the "Church of Rome ... corrupted the Sacrament of the Lord's Supper and befouled the doctrine thereof" by the "vagary" and "false doctrine ... that the bread and wine administered as emblems of Christ's flesh and blood in the Sacrament of the Lord's Supper are transmuted by priestly consecration into the actual flesh and blood of Jesus Christ".[4] Elder Bruce R. McConkie, with considerably less tact, taught that "the 'Real Presence' of Christ" was "one of the most obviously false, absurd, and ridiculous doctrines espoused" by the Catholic Church (for Elder McConkie, there were, of course, any number of such doctrines).[5]

[4] James E. Talmage, *Jesus the Christ: A Study of the Messiah and His Mission according to Holy Scriptures Both Ancient and Modern* (Salt Lake City: Deseret News, 1915), 748.

[5] Bruce R. McConkie, *Mormon Doctrine* (Salt Lake City: Bookcraft, 1958), 730.

Yet, without question, the first thing I read in the Church Fathers truly shook me concerned this teaching. The early Christian bishop and martyr Saint Ignatius of Antioch wrote a series of letters to several of the churches, around A.D. 107, while he was on his way as a captive to be executed at Rome. I was unsettled by the unusually realistic language he employed when describing the Eucharist. To the Romans, Saint Ignatius wrote that he "desire[d] the bread of God, the heavenly bread, the bread of life, which is the flesh of Jesus Christ, the Son of God, who became afterwards the seed of David and Abraham; and [he] desire[d] the drink of God, namely, His blood, which is incorruptible love and eternal life".[6] He counseled the Church of Philadelphia to "have but one Eucharist. For there is one flesh of our Lord Jesus Christ, and one cup to show forth the unity of His blood; one altar; as there is one bishop".[7] But his letters to the Church of Smyrna, where his friend Saint Polycarp was bishop, left little doubt what Saint Ignatius believed and what he supposed his readers to believe. Saint Ignatius warns the Christians of Smyrna not to associate with the Docetists—a group claiming that Jesus did not actually become flesh, but that he only *appeared* that way, when in fact he was a divine spirit. Saint Ignatius counseled his flock to stay away from Docetists, who "abstain from the Eucharist ... *because they confess not the Eucharist to be the flesh of our Saviour Jesus Christ*".[8] His characterization of the reasons for the Docetists' refusal to

---

[6] Ignatius of Antioch, *Epistle to the Romans*, chap. 7, in *Ante-Nicene Fathers*, ed. Alexander Roberts and James Donaldson, vol. 1 (New York: Charles Scribner and Sons, 1999).

[7] Ignatius of Antioch, *Epistle to the Philadelphians*, chap. 4, in *Ante-Nicene Fathers*, vol. 1.

[8] Ignatius of Antioch, *Epistle to the Smyrnaeans*, in *Ante-Nicene Fathers*, vol. 1 (emphasis mine).

confess that the Eucharist is the Flesh of Jesus left little doubt to me that Saint Ignatius and the Church of Smyrna believed in the Real Presence. And as I contemplated the dating of these letters and the likely age at which Saint Ignatius suffered martyrdom, the raw antiquity of the belief was evident to me. Saint Ignatius' writings were not introducing a new concept or innovation, but speaking of something he expected his audience to understand and believe already—something they all took for granted. Moreover, quite apart from the Catholic tradition (in my view reasonable) that Saint Ignatius was acquainted with some of the apostles, more important still was the simple fact that he was their late contemporary and they were within his living memory. It seemed quite reasonable to me to believe that pre-existing views held by someone of that age—likely an old man already by the *early* second century—were the closest I would get to the beliefs of the apostles.

But nothing had an effect quite like the following passage, which I came upon as I was reading through the text of Saint Justin Martyr's *First Apology*, a document written in Rome around A.D. 155, in which Saint Justin explains to his non-Christian audience what the Christians of Rome do on Sundays. He taught:

This food is called among us Εὐχαριστία [the Eucharist], of which no one is allowed to partake but the man who believes that the things which we teach are true, and who has been washed with the washing that is for the remission of sins, and unto regeneration, and who is so living as Christ has enjoined. For not as common bread and common drink do we receive these; but in like manner as Jesus Christ our Saviour, having been made flesh by the Word of God, had both flesh and blood for our salvation, so likewise have we been taught that the food which is blessed by the prayer of His word, and from which our blood and flesh by transmutation are nourished, is the flesh and blood of that Jesus who was made flesh.[9]

The teachings of subsequent Fathers from all over the Christian world in the following decades and centuries—from Saint Irenaeus of Lyon to Tertullian to Saint Hippolytus to Saint Cyprian of Carthage to Saint Ephraim the Syriac to Saint Cyril of Jerusalem to Saint Ambrose of Milan to Saint Cyril of Alexandria—were consistent. Whether I liked it or not, the belief was just so palpable and present, it was hard for me to ignore the sense that even an idiosyncratic personal Christianity would fail to be Christianity in any meaningful sense if it left this belief out of the mix. It was so consistent that cutting ties with the belief appeared to me to border on cutting ties with Christianity itself.

As I read later on that year, while diving through numerous commentaries on the Church Fathers and early Christianity, even Protestant scholars like J. N. D. Kelly admitted that early Christians "clearly ... intend[ed] [the] realism" in their description of the Eucharist "to be taken strictly".[10] Jaroslav Pelikan—a scholar of early Christianity and Lutheran minister who would later convert to Eastern Orthodoxy—similarly wrote, as a Protestant, that "no orthodox father" of the Church ever denied the Real Presence or "declared the presence of the body and blood of Christ in the Eucharist to be no more than symbolic".[11] The Fathers stated "in strikingly realistic language" that

[9] Justin Martyr, The First Apology, chap. 66, in Ante-Nicene Fathers, vol. 1.

[10] J. N. D. Kelly, Early Christian Doctrines, rev. ed. (San Francisco: HarperSanFrancisco, 1978), 197–98.

[11] Jaroslav Pelikan, The Christian Tradition, A History of the Development of Doctrine: Emergence of the Catholic Tradition (100–600) (Chicago: University of Chicago Press, 1971), 1:167.

the bread and wine are indeed the Flesh and Blood of Christ after the Consecration.[12] The "doctrine of the real presence", while not expressed in the systematized theological terms and language of the sixteenth century (that is, "transubstantiation") "was already believed by the church" by the *end* of the first century A.D.[13] If I was going to call myself a Christian, I had to accept this belief. And I knew that this belief was held—not exclusively but quite famously—by the Catholic Church.

Another issue of importance to me was what appeared to be sufficiently clear and early support for a definition of the Trinity that, if it was not the precise doctrinal definition, was obviously close and in the camp of traditional Christian belief about God. I also realized that I had never taken the time to understand what Christians meant in the first place when they spoke about this complex doctrine. Rather, for my whole life I had seen a caricaturized version of this doctrine, presented as "pagan" in origin and manifestly nonsensical. Contempt for the doctrine of the Trinity has deep roots in Mormonism. Once Joseph Smith decided to cast it aside, he ridiculed it, teaching: "Many men say there is one God—the Father, the Son, and the Holy Ghost, are only one God! I say, that is a strange God anyhow—three in one, and one in three! It is a curious organization.... All are to be crammed into one God according to sectarianism; it would make the biggest God in all the world; he would be a wonderful big God; he would be a giant or a monster."[14]

[12] Pelikan, *Christian Tradition*, 1:167.

[13] Pelikan, *Christian Tradition*, 1:168.

[14] "History, 1838–1856, volume F-1 [1 May 1844–8 August 1844]", p. 103, Joseph Smith Papers, Church History Library of the Church of Jesus Christ of Latter-day Saints in Salt Lake City, Utah, https://www.josephsmithpapers.org/paper-summary/history-1838-1856-volume-f-1-1-may-1844-8-august-1844/109.

Apostle James Talmage, in the early twentieth century, said of the Nicene and Athanasian Creeds, "It would be difficult to conceive of a greater number of inconsistencies and contradictions expressed in words as few."[15] To this day, prominent Mormon leaders gently mock the doctrine in comparison to the supposedly "simple" henotheism of Mormonism. Apostle Russell Ballard told an audience in Argentina in 2014, "If people have a Catholic background, they don't know who God is. They don't know who the Savior is. Nor do they know who the Holy Ghost is."[16] Apostle Jeffrey Holland quoted portions of the Athanasian creed, which calls God's essence "incomprehensible", before a conference of new mission presidents in 2013, and quipped, "We agree with our critics on at least that point—that such a formulation for divinity is incomprehensible", stating that Mormons are "very comfortable, frankly, in letting it be known that we do not hold a fourth- or fifth-century, pagan-influenced view of the Godhead, and neither did those first Christian Saints who were eyewitnesses of the living Christ".[17] My own reading quickly disabused me of beliefs I had held in consequence of a lifetime of such trite polemics.

Saint Ignatius of Antioch, just after the turn of the second century, called "Jesus Christ our Lord" "God existing in flesh".[18] Commenting on the glory of the Cross to the Ephesians, Saint Ignatius refers to *"our God, Jesus*

[15] James E. Talmage, *The Articles of Faith*, 12th ed. (Salt Lake City: Deseret Book, 1987), 48.

[16] M. Russell Ballard, "Address to Young Single Adults" (Buenos Aires, Argentina, February 20, 2014), https://www.youtube.com/watch?v=qj7VgNDm7r0.

[17] Jeffrey R. Holland, "Knowing the Godhead", *Ensign,* January 2016, https://www.lds.org/ensign/2016/01/knowing-the-godhead?lang=eng.

[18] Ignatius of Antioch, *Epistle to the Ephesians*, chap. 7, in *Ante-Nicene Fathers*, vol. 1.

Christ, [who] was, according to the appointment *of God*, conceived in the womb by Mary, of the seed of David, but by the *Holy Ghost*."[19] Note the curiousness of this phrasing. Saint Ignatius recognizes Jesus Christ himself as the God of the Christians, yet acknowledges that Jesus was conceived in Mary's womb by the Holy Ghost by the appointment *of God*. Saint Ignatius does not mean God the Father appointed himself to be born of Mary— that much is apparent. Saint Ignatius presupposes a difference between the Father and Jesus, yet insists Jesus is God, while there is only one God. He elaborates elsewhere that those who "were persecuted, being inspired by his grace fully to convince the unbelieving that *there is one God, who is manifested himself by Jesus Christ his son, who is his eternal word [Logos]*."[20] Here, again, Saint Ignatius makes it clear that he believes "there is one God" and Jesus Christ is his *logos*, hearkening back to the introduction to the Gospel of John, which famously says, "In the beginning was *the Word*, and the Word was with God, and the Word *was God*."

Saint Justin Martyr's *Dialogue with Trypho the Jew* was further evidence to my mind of the deep and early roots of trinitarian belief. Saint Justin does not really discuss the Holy Spirit much (indeed, hardly any Christian writer does until after the Council of Nicaea and during the lead-up to the Council of Constantinople, in which the divinity of the Holy Spirit was affirmed). Saint Justin is focused on the Father and the Son, but he clearly expressed—to my satisfaction—at least what you might call a "binitarian" relationship between them.

[19] Ignatius of Antioch, *Epistle to the Ephesians*, chap. 18 (emphasis mine).
[20] Ignatius of Antioch, *Epistle to the Magnesians*, in *Ante-Nicene Fathers*, vol. 1 (emphasis mine).

In this treatise, set forth as a dialogue between Justin and a Jewish interlocutor who is challenging Christianity, Saint Justin extensively expounds how it is that Christians are monotheists but at the same time affirm that Jesus is divine, a seeming impossibility. Saint Justin's dialogue is filled with declarations that Christ is God. Trypho, however, criticizes Saint Justin's argument, saying that "when you say that this Christ existed as God before the ages, then that he submitted to be born to become a man, yet that he is not man of man, this assertion appears to me to be not merely paradoxical, but also foolish."[21] Saint Justin assures Trypho of Christ's divinity by declaring him to be God's *Logos* (Word), a word pregnant with meaning and a clear reference back to the Jewish Wisdom literature in which God's own rational principle in his own mind is one with God the Father, yet a distinct person.

Saint Justin explains, in some detail, that "God begat before all creatures a Beginning, who was a certain rational power proceeding from himself, who is called by the Holy Spirit, now the Glory of the Lord, now the Son, again Wisdom, again an Angel, then God, and then Lord and Logos." In a similar way to "when we get out some word, we begat the word" in our mind, and it comes forth from us, "yet not by abscission, so as to lessen the word which remains in us", so is the relationship between the Father and the Son. "As we see also happening in the case of a fire, which is not lessened when it has kindled [another], but remains the same."[22] At the same time, he is emphatic that "there will be no other God, O Trypho, nor was there from eternity any other existing ... but He who made and disposed all this universe. Nor do we think

[21] Justin Martyr, *Dialogue with Trypho*, chap. 48, in *Ante-Nicene Fathers*, vol. 1.
[22] Justin Martyr, *Dialogue with Trypho*, chap. 61.

that there is one God for us, another for you, but that He alone is God who led your fathers out from Egypt with a strong hand and a high arm. Nor have we trusted in any other (for there is no other), but in Him in whom you also have trusted, the God of Abraham, and of Isaac, and of Jacob."[23]

Saint Irenaeus of Lyon held a similar view, expounding on the idea that Jesus is the divine Logos (also teaching the divinity of the Holy Spirit). For Saint Irenaeus, "Christ Jesus [is] our Lord, and God, and Savior, and King."[24] Yet Saint Irenaeus was unequivocal in his monotheism, not least because he was arguing against the Gnostic sects who had an esoteric cosmology with any number of gods superior to the God of Israel—a God whom they believed to be evil. Saint Irenaeus was clear that there were not "numerous unlimited creators and gods, who begin from each other, and end in each other on every side."[25] Rather, the Christians "confess at once that which is true: this God, the Creator, who formed the world, is the only God, and that there is no other God besides him".[26] For Saint Irenaeus, "the Word, namely the Son, was always with the Father; and that Wisdom also, which is the Spirit, was present with Him, anterior to all creation."[27] But "there is ... one God."[28]

Athenagoras of Athens, in his plea for the Christians in A.D. 177, affirmed the divinity of God the Father, the Son, and the Holy Spirit, but—particularly given the fact

---

[23] Justin Martyr, *Dialogue with Trypho*, chap. 11.

[24] Irenaeus of Lyon, *Against Heresies*, bk. 1, chap. 10, no. 1, in *Ante-Nicene Fathers*, vol. 1.

[25] Irenaeus of Lyon, *Against Heresies*, bk. 2, chap. 1, no. 5.

[26] Irenaeus of Lyon, *Against Heresies*, bk. 4, chap. 32, no. 1.

[27] Irenaeus of Lyon, *Against Heresies*, bk. 4, chap. 20, no. 3.

[28] Irenaeus of Lyon, *Against Heresies*, bk. 4, chap. 20, no. 4.

that he was dealing with a pagan Greek-influenced audience—he was equally clear, in his chapter entitled "Absurdities of Polytheism", that believing in the divinity of these Three *was not* a belief in "two or more gods".[29] Athenagoras quoted extensively from Isaiah and the verses affirming that there is only one God, and there is no other besides him. According to Athenagoras, Christians

> acknowledge one God, uncreated, eternal, invisible, impassable, incomprehensible, illimitable, who is apprehended by understanding only in the reason, who is encompassed by the light, and beauty, and spirit, and power ineffable, by whom the universe has been created through His Logos.... I say His Logos, for we acknowledge also a Son of God.... But the Son of God is the Logos of the Father, in idea and in operation; for after the pattern of Him and by Him were all things made, Father and the Son being one. And, the Son being in the Father and the Father in the Son, in oneness and power of spirit the Understanding and Reason of the Father is the Son of God.... The Holy Spirit himself also, which operates in the prophets, we assert to be an effluence of God, flowing from him, and returning back again like a beam of the sun. Who, then, would not be astonished to hear men who speak of God the Father, and of God the Son, and of the Holy Spirit, and who declare both their power and union and their distinction in order, called atheist?[30]

For Athenagoras, Christians "acknowledge a God, and a Son His Logos, and a Holy Spirit, united in essence,— the Father, the Son, the Spirit, because the Son is the

---

[29] Athenagoras of Athens, *A Plea for the Christians*, chap. 8, in *Ante-Nicene Fathers*, vol. 2.

[30] Athenagoras of Athens, *Plea for the Christians*, chap. 10.

intelligence, reason, wisdom of the Father, and the Spirit an effluence, as light from fire".[31] But, he is clear, "there is one God."[32]

Later research provided important, and ultimately confirming, context to these teachings about the nature of God. Jesus was a Jew. His earliest followers were Jews. And they believed in the Jewish faith that existed in their time—second-temple Judaism. There is no doubt about the strict monotheism of that time. It was not, as some Mormon writers assert, a belief that there are many gods, only one of which (our Heavenly Father) may be worshiped. No. To Jesus and the Jews of this time, there *is* only one God—the God of Israel.

This strict monotheism is summarized in the ever-important Shema Yisrael of Deuteronomy 6:4: "Hear O Israel, the LORD our God is one LORD." As Mormon writer Boyd Kirkland observed, "As a Jewish male, Jesus would have been taught from his youth to recite the *Shema* at least twice daily ... this liturgical creed was understood to be a confession of monotheism, that is, there is no other God than Jehovah."[33] "Jesus himself accepted Jewish monotheism", and "the New Testament contains no evidence that he ever taught his disciples of a God superior to Jehovah, the God of Israel."[34]

On a certain occasion, a lawyer asks Jesus which is the greatest commandment. Jesus responds with the Shema: "Jesus answered, 'The first is, "*Hear, O Israel: The Lord our God, the Lord is one;* and you shall love the Lord your God with all your heart, and with all your soul, and with all

---

[31] Athenagoras of Athens, *Plea for the Christians*, chap. 24.

[32] Athenagoras of Athens, *Plea for the Christians*, chap. 7.

[33] Boyd Kirkland, "Elohim and Jehovah in Mormonism and the Bible", *Dialogue: A Journal of Mormon Thought* 19, no. 1 (Spring 1986): 85.

[34] Kirkland, "Elohim and Jehovah", 84.

your mind, and with all your strength" ' " (Mk 12:29–30).
As Kirkland concludes, "The uncompromising monotheism of the *Shema* was equally fundamental to the Christian.... Paul essentially Christianized the *Shema* when he
wrote, 'There is none other God but one.... To us there
is but one God.' "[35]

As I read through the Church Fathers and saw them
affirming both that Jesus is "God" and that that he is distinct from "the Father"—while at the same time professing
monotheism and defending Christians against charges of
polytheism—it dawned on me that there were solid theological grounds for the technical language later employed
to describe *how it is* that there is only one God—a nonne-
gotiable to the early Christians—and yet Jesus is *also* God.
These, and any number of other teachings of the Fathers,
forced me into an intellectual humility about Christian
belief. It did not take long for me to realize that my own
concepts of God (as taught to me by Mormonism) were
in fact alien to Christianity. Whether I understood the
Trinity or not was beside the point. I had to acknowledge
the exceptional antiquity of the belief, as it seemed plainly
reflected in the writings of Christians of the early second
century, and that it was not any sort of novel belief for
them, but one they had inherited from the Christian communities to which they belonged, pushing the belief—in
its core, if not in its linguistic articulation—back even further in time.

Later scholarly reading confirmed what I had seen with
my own eyes in the Fathers but, shockingly, pushed those
beliefs back even *earlier*. One of the leading scholars on
ancient Christian devotion to Jesus, the late Dr. Larry
Hurtado, persuasively drew a conclusion that reshaped
early Christian studies, which was once enamored with

---

[35] Kirkland, "Elohim and Jehovah", 84.

the idea that the divinity of Jesus was a late first- or probably early-second-century development: that "devotion to
Jesus as divine erupted suddenly and quickly, not gradually
and late, among first-century circles of followers."[36]

"The binitarian devotional pattern began so early that
no trace is left of any stages of development.... It is necessary to attribute the origins of the cultic reverence to
Christ to Aramaic-speaking and Greek-speaking circles,
and to the first years of the Christian movement (the
30s)."[37] The spread of this belief about Jesus' divinity—and
his relation to the Father—happened so quickly after Jesus'
death, there was simply no room for it to be the result of
an "apostasy", for it was a belief of the apostolic age. The
belief is "astonishingly early" and occurred as "a virtual
explosion.... So far as historical inquiry permits us to say,
it was an immediate feature of the circles of those who
identified themselves with reference to [Jesus]."[38]

As Hurtado put it, "Only a certain wishful thinking
continues to attribute the reverence of Jesus as divine
decisively to the influence of pagan religion and the influx
of Gentile converts."[39] The earliest Christians were clearly
"influenced" by "Jewish tradition", particularly "in their
critique of pagan polytheism" and rejection of it.[40] And
"like their Jewish coreligionists, [the earliest Christians]
came to draw selectively upon philosophical traditions"
in their explanation of the relationship between God the
Father and Jesus, "but in the earliest centuries they did so
with considerable caution."[41]

---

[36] Larry Hurtado, *Lord Jesus Christ: Devotion to Jesus in Earliest Christianity*
(Grand Rapids, MI: William B. Eerdmans Publishing, 2003), 650.

[37] Hurtado, *Lord Jesus Christ*, 136.

[38] Hurtado, *Lord Jesus Christ*, 2.

[39] Hurtado, *Lord Jesus Christ*, 650.

[40] Hurtado, *Lord Jesus Christ*, 651.

[41] Hurtado, *Lord Jesus Christ*, 651.

The earliest Christians "stridently professed sole allegiance to the God of the Old Testament, their exclusivist monotheism sometimes being tested by the threat of death".[42] Yet "they also posited a real and radical plurality" within God that "reshap[ed] ... the monotheism inherited from the Jewish biblical tradition, initially taking things in a 'binitarian' direction" and later, "a trinitarian model".[43]

The idea, embedded in me from my Mormon faith, that the Trinity was some kind of outgrowth of pagan philosophy invading true Christianity simply crumbled apart. Indeed, it struck me as ironic that the Mormon faith insisted that the Trinity was a pagan idea while espousing a plurality of material gods who copulate with one another to bear spirit children eternally who can then later reach this phase of godhood. The coherency of the Trinity, I would later come to accept with time and study of the Church's intellectual tradition and exposition of the doctrine; but the antiquity of the traditional conception of God was irrefutable to my mind.

One final, and somewhat related, discovery is worth mentioning. It is an indispensable Mormon doctrine that shortly after the death of the apostles, there was a Great Apostasy, and the true Gospel—that is, Mormonism—as well as the "priesthood" was taken from the Earth until they were restored through Joseph Smith. The most influential articulation of this teaching is without doubt the 1909 book by Elder James Talmage, *The Great Apostasy Considered in Light of the Scriptural and Secular History.* As Elder Talmage put it, "We affirm that with the passing of the so-called apostolic age the Church gradually drifted into a condition of apostasy, whereby succession

[42] Hurtado, *Lord Jesus Christ,* 2.
[43] Hurtado, *Lord Jesus Christ,* 2.

in the priesthood was broken; and that the Church, as an earthly organization operating under divine direction and having authority to officiate in spiritual ordinances, ceased to exist."[44] Elder Talmage rightly argued that it is in fact "obvious" that the Great Apostasy is "a condition precedent to the re-establishment of the Church in modern times.... If the alleged apostasy of the primitive Church was not a reality, The Church of Jesus Christ of Latter-day Saints is not the divine institution its name proclaims",[45] because "such restoration and re-establishment, with the modern bestowal of the Holy Priesthood, would be unnecessary and indeed impossible had the Church of Christ continued among men with unbroken succession of Priesthood and power, since the 'meridian of time.' "[46] Thus, establishing a Great Apostasy was "a question of the utmost importance" for him.[47]

I was not looking for such a thing to begin with, but incidental to my reading of the Church Fathers, it dawned on me that there was about as much evidence of the existence of Mormons in the first few centuries of Christianity as there was of the existence of Nephites and Lamanites in America—which is to say none that could lead to a reasonable conclusion of their reality. Everywhere I looked, there were descriptions and refutations and rebuttals of all manner of competing visions of Christianity—from Judaizers to Ebionites, Docetists to Gnostics, Marcionites to Montanists, Seballians to Arians—but no Mormons. Indeed, there was nothing that remotely resembled Mormonism. What I saw was one recognizable group fighting strenuously

[44] James E. Talmage, *The Great Apostasy Considered in the Light of Scriptural and Secular History* (Salt Lake City: Deseret News, 1909), 18–19.

[45] Talmage, *Great Apostasy*, iii.

[46] Talmage, *Great Apostasy*, iii.

[47] Talmage, *Great Apostasy*, 18.

against these various other groups and claiming to teach the true faith that ultimately won out—and the group looked a lot to me like Catholicism or Orthodoxy. Far from a church that operated in expectation of apostasy, the Christians I saw appeared to expect that their religion was going according to a plan set forth by the apostles themselves. And there did appear to me to be something special about one church in particular: the Church of Rome.

One of the earliest non–New Testament writings—indeed, an epistle that only barely missed being considered canonical and part of the New Testament itself—is known as the *Epistle of Clement of Rome to the Corinthians*, often shortened to *First Clement*. Some scholars debate whether Saint Clement himself wrote it (because it was published as being from the "Church of Rome" and not Saint Clement personally), but as long as there is record of the document, it has uniformly been attributed to Clement. Early tradition identified Saint Clement with the Clement mentioned in Philippians as one of Saint Paul's "fellow workers, whose names are in the book of life" (Phil 4:3). Saint Clement's writing is most definitely influenced by a Pauline style, and it is possible he is one and the same. But whether one believes this tradition or not is ultimately beside the point, because it seemed to me at the time that Saint Clement's proximity to the apostles was difficult to deny.

The epistle is usually dated in the 90s A.D., well within living memory of those who knew Jesus, and before the date usually ascribed to the death of Saint John the Apostle. The epistle speaks with a striking present-ness about the apostles: "The *apostles have preached the Gospel* to us from the Lord Jesus Christ."[48] And when exhorting the

---

[48] Clement of Rome, *Epistle to the Corinthians*, chap. 42, in *Ante-Nicene Fathers*, vol. 1 (emphasis mine).

Corinthians to faithfulness, the author observes that he need "not . . . dwell upon ancient examples", such as Moses or David, but could point "to the most recent spiritual heroes", "the noble examples *of our own generation*", and more specifically, the "greatest and most righteous pillars" of the Church of Rome, Peter and Paul, who were "persecuted and put to death".[49] As with Saint Ignatius' writings on the Eucharist, the dating and location of Clement's epistle struck me, as its author and audience are all squarely within living memory of the apostles.

The purpose of the letter was to respond to an earlier request sent by the Church of Corinth to the Church of Rome, asking the latter to settle an important ecclesial controversy at Corinth: whether the Corinthian lay people could depose their leaders. Despite other prestigious churches located at a similar distance, such as Smyrna and Ephesus—each with strong apostolic character—the Corinthians appealed to the Church of Rome. Saint Clement, writing for the Church of Rome, responded no; they could do no such thing.

He explained, "The apostles have preached the Gospel to us from the Lord Jesus Christ"; Christ was "sent forth by God and the apostles by Christ". Such "appointments" were "according to the will of God". The apostles then "went forth" into the world preaching, and they in turn "appointed the first-fruits [of their labors], having first proved them by the Spirit, to be bishops and deacons of those who should afterwards believe".[50] The Corinthian Christians could not undo that. According to Clement, "Our apostles also knew, through our Lord Jesus Christ, and there would be strife on account of the office of the

---

[49] Clement, *Epistle to the Corinthians*, chap. 5 (emphasis mine).
[50] Clement, *Epistle to the Corinthians*, chap. 42.

episcopate," and therefore "they appointed those [ministers] already mentioned, and afterwards gave instructions, that when these should fall asleep, other approved men should succeed them in their ministry." The Church of Rome therefore declared "that those appointed by them, or afterwards by other eminent men ... cannot be justly dismissed from the ministry".[51]

By Clement's account, these early Christian bishops had been appointed by the apostles themselves, sometimes even ahead of time, to keep the faith and lead the Church. I later learned that my edition of Clement was, as discussed in a footnote in that edition, missing a large section in the manuscript that was used. Other editions, however, include this section, and the authoritative sense of the Roman Church in the author is even stronger in the portion that was missing from my own reading: "But should any disobey what has been said by [Jesus Christ] through us, let them understand that they will entangle themselves in transgression and no small danger. But for our part we shall be innocent of this sin."[52] As Roger E. Olson candidly comments in *The Story of Christian Theology*, which is self-consciously told from a Protestant perspective, while *First Clement* may not be enough to show the concept of the papacy as we know it today, Clement of Rome undoubtably "seems to have had a consciousness of special responsibility and authority that may have stemmed from the idea of apostolic succession", given that he was "the bishop of Rome—the successor of Peter and Paul".[53]

My reading of Saint Ignatius of Antioch's writings only strengthened the sense of tight connection between the

---

[51] Clement, *Epistle to the Corinthians*, chap. 44.

[52] Clement, *Epistle to the Corinthians*, chap. 59.

[53] Roger E. Olson, *The Story of Christian Theology: Twenty Centuries of Tradition and Reform* (Westmont, IL: InterVarsity Press, 1999), 44.

apostles and these early Christian writers and bishops. Saint
Ignatius repeatedly exhorted the Ephesians to be "subject
to the bishop and the presbytery".[54] He taught that it was
"fitting that ye should run together in accordance with the
will of your bishop, which thing also ye do. For your justly
renowned presbytery, worthy of God, is fitted as exactly
to the bishop as the strings are to the harp."[55] He noted
that the Christians of Ephesus were at that time "joined to
[the bishop] as the Church is to Jesus Christ, and as Jesus
Christ is to the Father", warning: "Let us be careful, then,
not to set ourselves in opposition to the bishop in order
that we may be subject to God."[56] The bishop was to
be received as the one "whom the Master of the house
sends to be over His household, as we would do Him that
sent him".[57] In his letter to the Magnesians, Saint Ignatius
exhorts the Church there to "divine harmony, while your
bishop presides in the place of God".[58] To the Trallians, he
counseled that in fact, "apart from [bishops, presbyters, and
deacons] there is no Church."[59] And most shocking to me
of all, by far, was his letter to the Smyrnaens: "Wherever
the bishop shall appear, there let the multitude also be; even
as wherever Jesus Christ is, *there is the Catholic Church*"[60]—a
name for the Church that Saint Ignatius, already likely an
old man in A.D. 107, took for granted was in accepted use
among all seven churches to which he wrote.

[54] Ignatius of Antioch, *Epistle to the Ephesians*, chap. 2, in *Ante-Nicene Fathers*, vol. 1.

[55] Ignatius of Antioch, *Epistle to the Ephesians*, chap. 4.

[56] Ignatius of Antioch, *Epistle to the Ephesians*, chap. 5.

[57] Ignatius of Antioch, *Epistle to the Ephesians*, chap. 6.

[58] Ignatius of Antioch, *Epistle to the Magnesians*, chap. 6, in *Ante-Nicene Fathers*, vol. 1.

[59] Ignatius of Antioch, *Epistle to the Trallians*, chap. 3, in *Ante-Nicene Fathers*, vol. 1.

[60] Ignatius of Antioch, *Epistle to the Smyrnaeans*, chap. 8, in *Ante-Nicene Fathers*, vol. 1 (emphasis mine).

A turning point for me, however, came when I finally arrived at the writings of Saint Irenaeus of Lyon. Saint Irenaeus was an Eastern Christian from Smyrna (now Izmir, Turkey), who was eventually transplanted to the West, to what is modern-day Lyon, France, in the late second century. During Saint Irenaeus' time, an esoteric version of Christianity, called Gnosticism, began to become popular throughout the Roman Empire. *Gnosis* is Greek for "knowledge", and these various groups emphasized salvation through secret knowledge, allegedly handed down through only a select *few* of the apostles and hidden from others. Gnostics were also characterized by their hatred of all things physical and bodily and the view that salvation would consist of being entirely free from the body in a purely spiritual form. They had an immensely complex cosmology, believing in hundreds of god-like "emanations" and "aeons". Reading through Saint Irenaeus' exhaustive recitation of the beliefs of the Gnostics is not for the faint of heart—it is a bewildering peek into a religion with no precise parallel today. But because of its popularity and its claim to be secretly endorsed by some of the apostles, Saint Irenaeus decided to write a public refutation of the entire system of belief.

One of his main lines of argumentation was simple: the secretive Gnostic views are contrary to the public apostolic faith that had been handed down by the bishops of the Church, each of whom can trace his ordination back to the apostles and the apostolic age. "The Catholic Church possesses one and the same faith throughout the whole world"[61] and "received this tradition from the apostles".[62] Thus, the sure guide to staying true to Christianity, for

---

[61] Irenaeus, *Against Heresies*, bk. 1, chap. 10, no. 3.
[62] Irenaeus, *Against Heresies*, bk. 2, chap. 9, no. 1.

Saint Irenaeus, was the "tradition which originates from the apostles, [and] which is preserved by means of the successions of presbyters in the Churches".[63]

This same faith held by Saint Irenaeus was that held by Saint Polycarp, who "was not only instructed by apostles, and conversed with many who had seen Christ, but was also, by apostles in Asia, appointed bishop of the Church in Smyrna, whom [Saint Irenaeus] also saw in [his] early youth" and whom he heard teach "things which he had learned from the apostles".[64] (Saint Polycarp and Saint Ignatius of Antioch, also by tradition ordained by apostles, were acquainted with one another and corresponded.)

But most important of all, and most jarring to me, was Saint Irenaeus' argument that rather than "reckon up the successions of all the churches" from the apostles, which "would be very tedious", he could "put to confusion all those" who taught contrary to this faith, by a singular example: the faith "of the very great, the very ancient, and universally known Church founded and organized at Rome by the two most glorious apostles, Peter and Paul.... For *it is a matter of necessity that every church should agree with this Church, on account of its preeminent authority.*"[65] Those words, I have later learned, are a matter of hot dispute, and you can probably tell why. In the margin, I simply wrote, "Wow".

Other issues that caught my attention could be noted, including early references to the practice of venerating saints and their remains, the prominent place the Virgin Mary occupied in salvation history, and the descriptions of Christian liturgical practices. The more I read, the more

---

[63] Irenaeus, *Against Heresies*, bk. 3, chap. 2, no. 2.

[64] Irenaeus, *Against Heresies*, bk. 3, chap. 3, no. 4.

[65] Irenaeus, *Against Heresies*, bk. 3, chap. 3, no. 2.

I saw in Newman's famous observation, "This one thing at least is certain; whatever history teaches, whatever it omits, whatever it exaggerates or extenuates, whatever it says and unsays, at least the Christianity of history is not Protestantism. If ever there were a safe truth, it is this ... to be deep in history is to cease to be a Protestant."[66]

I WANT TO BE CLEAR, however, about exactly what I am saying I saw and what I am *not* saying I saw in early Christian history. I did not see at that time every jot and tittle of Catholicism, and there are a host of views espoused by a number of Fathers that are not Catholic teaching. You would be hard pressed to find elaborate Marian devotion fully articulated in the first two centuries of Christianity. That was not the point, however. There was to my mind a certain thrust to what I read, and that thrust was Catholic rather than something else. I saw no Mormons, nor did I see people who saw salvation as something that cannot be lost or the Scriptures as the sole and sufficient rule of faith.

So how was it that I could find identity between the "Catholic Church" of Saint Ignatius and Saint Irenaeus and the Catholic Church of today? That came in two ways: first, it came through my growing familiarity with the intellectual tradition of the Catholic Church and what she said about herself; second, it came by falling in love with the beauty in her, primarily the beauty of her ancient liturgy and her artistic and spiritual patrimony.

On New Year's Eve, 2017, I purchased a multipart video series called *Catholicism* that had been produced by, at the time of its release, Father Robert Barron of

---

[66] Newman, *An Essay on the Development of Christian Doctrine*, intro.

Chicago—Bishop Barron by the time I watched it. Only a few weeks later I purchased his follow-up series entitled *Catholicism: The Pivotal Players*. I had devoured both by the end of January 2018. In them I experienced something I had not experienced before. Bishop Barron made frequent reference to two of his spiritual and intellectual heroes, the great scholastic Church doctor Saint Thomas Aquinas and the English convert John Henry Newman. He introduced me to their thinking—and by extension, the thought of the Church—on a range of important topics that appealed, for the first time any religion had done so, to my intellect.

So contrary to my previous experience, I found a religion that—while my own upbringing had taught me it was among the most backward, superstitious, and repressive in the world—was in reality unafraid of itself and unafraid of reason. Indeed, while Mormonism had taught me that I had been made in the image of God in the sense that like him, I had fingers and toes and eyes and ears, this religion taught something that resonated with me in a way so deep I find it hard to express adequately: mankind is made in God's image in the sense that he endowed us with *reason*—with an intellect and a will. Mankind, this faith told me, were animals, to be sure, but *rational* animals. Thus, what made us most like God, what could draw us closer to him, was our *intellect*.

Reading Saint Thomas Aquinas' famous "Five Ways" for demonstrating the existence of God was exhilarating, but nothing more so than the very beginning of that section, in which Saint Thomas boldly begins with the question "Whether God exists" and sets forth two of the most enduring and potent arguments *against* God's existence there are—the problem of evil and the fact that the natural world can be explained without reference to God. Saint Thomas, in answering these objections head on, also firmly rejects one of the most famous arguments for God's existence there is—the "ontological" argument developed by Saint Anselm of Canterbury—as clearly inadequate. The entire scene—a medieval saint beginning his treatise with questioning whether there is even a God at all and setting forward robust versions of the best arguments against God, criticizing another famous saint's argument for God's existence while he is at it—was, to say the least, refreshing.

When I finally turned to John Henry Newman's *Essay on the Development of Christian Doctrine* in earnest, I saw an intellectual acuity unparalleled in my prior faith, as well as an honesty. At the time I began familiarizing myself with his works, he was Blessed John Henry Newman, not yet recognized a saint by the Church, but he was on his way (he was canonized on October 13, 2019). His exalted status in the Church was, to my mind, a striking endorsement of his approach to Church history and doctrine. Here was someone who acknowledged, frankly, that many important Catholic beliefs, as far as the historical record permits us to judge, developed over time from earlier beliefs. Yet this was no strike against Catholicism, but in fact a strong argument in favor of it. Newman cogently set forth criteria for determining legitimate versus illegitimate developments in Church teaching and brilliantly articulated the historical continuity between the Church of the first centuries and that of the later ones as being like the identity that exists between an acorn and an oak tree. They are different, yet the same in the most fundamental and important way. The latter is merely the natural fruition of the former. So, too, the dogmas of the Catholic Church. The faith was indeed once delivered to the Church, but Newman's exposition on just what that means utterly captivated me—perhaps all the more so because I had left a tradition that had not really found a coherent and mature way to deal with its history.

I began purchasing and reading books on philosophy and the Christian intellectual tradition, which continued to persuade me of the alarming reasonableness of the Christian faith, and the Catholic tradition specifically. But there was a second, simultaneous factor that began to move me ever closer to Rome: her tradition of beauty as expressed in liturgical devotion, which began to lead me to what might be called mystical encounters with the God of Christianity. When I say mystical, I do not mean a visionary or supernatural phenomenon perceived with my eyes or ears; rather, there simply arose in me a *sense* of this Divine Being that was so drastically different from my previous relationship with God that it alarmed me.

The first of these personal devotions began by trying simply to accept that, for example, perhaps I had not really understood prayer. All my life, I had been taught that Jesus' instruction prior to the Our Father in the Sermon on the Mount was providing a *pattern* of free-form prayer and warning *against* recited prayer. Of course, that is not at all how the early Christian communities, or the giant body of Christendom for nearly two thousand years after that, viewed the matter. To be sure, free-form prayer is a part of that tradition, but the Church's prayer life was fundamentally corporate, fundamentally liturgical. As the early Christian writing known as the *Didache* teaches, "Thrice in the day" Christians are to pray, not as the hypocrites, "but as the Lord commanded in His Gospel",[67] quoting the Lord's Prayer from Matthew. So I began committing myself to memorized Catholic prayer at set times in the day. I purchased a rosary, as prayer beads were a longstanding devotional tool in traditional Christianity, East and West. As I noted in a later email to my wife, "The reason I got a

[67] *The Teaching of the Twelve Apostles*, chap. 8, in *Ante-Nicene Fathers*, vol. 7.

rosary was that I had a dream" in which she "told me get [a rosary] and keep it in my left pocket". "But it turns out," I noted, they are traditionally carried on the left side, to symbolize they are a spiritual weapon like a sword. I began carrying a rosary in my left pocket and have never stopped since. I bought candles, incense, and icons of Christ and the Virgin Mary and would spend a great deal of time alone in prayer looking at those images and thinking about this God to whom I was being introduced through Catholicism.

During one of the episodes of his video programs, Bishop Barron dedicated time to the famous sculpture by Michelangelo, the *Pietà*, which depicts the Virgin Mary with the body of her Son in her arms following the Crucifixion, her gaze cast down upon him, and her hands somewhat offering him to us. I was moved. I wept. Not at the scene depicted, or the concept it was attempting to display, but rather at the thought that I was beholding something truly *beautiful*. Not something that I just thought was beautiful, but something the beauty of which was virtually uncontested. If beauty is *real*, and not, as the saying goes, merely in the "eye of the beholder"—but if beauty is *real* and exists *outside* of me, where does it come from? What does it point to? If goodness is *real*, what does that mean and what does it point to? And who was this God Catholicism was talking about who does not *possess* the virtues of goodness, love, truth, beauty, and being, but who rather *was* Goodness *itself*, Love *itself*, Truth *itself*, Beauty *itself*, and Being *itself*? The more I thought about him, the more I began to understand the concept that, perhaps, God was truly incomprehensible—and truly awful, as the famous saying of Rabbi Abraham Heschel goes: "God is not nice, He is not an uncle. God is an earthquake."[68]

---

[68] Quoted in Jacob Needleman, *The New Religions* (London: Doubleday, 1970), 6.

This mysteriousness of the Christian God began to take a deeper hold of me as I inched my way into traditional Christian worship practices.

Near the beginning of 2018, my thoughts of actually becoming Catholic started slowly to become more serious as I continued to read through early Christian history and engage with a number of writings in favor of (and against) Catholicism. But it dawned on me that in all my life, I had never been to a Catholic Mass. I had been inside a few Catholic churches on my mission in Argentina, but I had never even really seen what traditional Christian liturgy looked like. For weeks, I would think out loud about going, and I began searching for Catholic parishes near me.

In my research on the current liturgy of the Catholic Church, I saw that there were at the time two accepted usages in the Roman Rite: the "ordinary form", which was, to simplify things greatly, the vernacular Mass promulgated as a reform in 1970 following the Second Vatican Council of the 1960s; and the "extraordinary form", the Mass that had been normative for some five hundred years following the Council of Trent, and that is offered in Latin (and that was indeed quite a bit older than that in substance—according to the preeminent scholar of the development of the Roman Rite, from the sixth century onward, "the permanent text" of the various parts of the Mass was "almost identical with present day usage" in 1949[69]). Naively unaware of the "liturgy wars" within Catholicism, I simply assumed the Church sensibly had two options, one in the vernacular that was more updated, and another that was its more ancient form. I figured, if I was going to see what Catholicism is like, I would go whole hog and try out the extraordinary form. It struck

---

[69] Joseph A. Jungmann, S.J., *The Mass of the Roman Rite: Its Origins and Development*, abridged ed. (Notre Dame, IN: Ave Maria Press, 2012), 1:49.

me as the Catholicism of my imagination all those years as a Mormon. I purchased a missal and watched some YouTube videos of a Latin Mass to try to get a sense of what it was all about. I decided to wait until after Easter, because the last thing I wanted was to show up on a "big day" and stick out.

On Sunday morning, May 13, 2018, I traveled the twenty- or thirty-minute drive from my home in Fairfax, Virginia, to Saint Rita Catholic Church in Alexandria dressed in my suit and tie, missal in hand, early and ready for the 9:30 A.M. Traditional Latin Mass. It was dark and quiet. Even as the pews filled, no one spoke to each other. Many, though not all, the women wore traditional chapel veils as they entered the church. People were lighting candles before a large statute of the Blessed Virgin Mary, crowned in gold and holding the Christ Child in her arms. The stained glass windows were filled with the morning light, putting on the impressive display for which they were designed. I sat in the very back row, put down a kneeler, and began to pray. After a while, at 9:30 on the dot, a bell rang out and everyone stood up. The schola began the beautiful Gregorian chants, which haunted me. The sweet smell of frankincense filled the entire room, and the colored light from the dazzling windows made visible rays through the dense clouds of smoke that wafted upward to heaven. There was an immense solemnity about the whole thing, and I felt as though I had been transported not only into another millennium, but into another world, and maybe another universe altogether.

The proceedings moved on, and I was quickly lost, unable to follow along in my missal, so I just watched and tried to do as everyone else did. Yet the matter was so foreign to me—not in a bad way, just shockingly different from anything I had experienced. I looked about the church, which was quiet enough that you could hear a pin drop, during the apex of the Mass when the Eucharist, just after the Consecration, is elevated on high by the priest. I pondered, stupefied, "Can it really be?" I was impressed by the devotion of those in attendance—a lot more people than I had expected, and a lot younger to boot. It was plain to me that, whatever else I personally believed about the Mass and the Eucharist, these people were worshiping God, and the whole ritual felt, to be sincere, like the first time in my entire life I had really seen and participated in worship. I do not mean in any way to denigrate the sincerity and devotion of Mormons; but I do wish to suggest that for me there was something almost palpably different about this worship—it was clear whom I was worshiping and *that* I was worshiping. For months, I attended Mass at 9:30 and made it home in time to go with my family to Sacrament meeting, and each Sunday the contrast became that much starker.

My wife encouraged my attendance at Mass, not because she wanted me to be Catholic, but because, from her perspective, her husband was slowly reemerging from the darkness that had enveloped him before. I found renewed purpose in my life, and in a real sense, a deeper one than I had before. I felt a more mature grounding in my faith and found myself in a different relationship to God than I had been before. Catholicism taught me new lessons about prayer, about suffering, about people. Still, I knew that becoming Catholic would require changes to my life, some of which would be difficult. And my own sense of having been deceived in my Mormon faith made me much more cautious in my approach to Catholicism and in forming my beliefs. Throughout 2017 and early 2018, I continued to research a number of options, including how to convert to Judaism, Eastern Orthodoxy, and

Lutheranism. But with time, I was ultimately drawn to the conclusion, on the intellectual side, that Catholicism was the historical inheritor of early Christianity, and that as between Catholicism and the only other contender I found to have a reasonable claim (Orthodoxy), I found on balance that Rome had the better side of the primary argument that sadly divides these two beautiful expressions of the apostolic faith: the primacy of the bishop of Rome.

Yet my decision to assent to the teachings of the Catholic Church did not come in a flash and trailed many months behind my conclusion that Catholicism was what it claimed to be. There was nothing exceptional about that experience. There were not any strong feelings involved either. Rather, we were on a family vacation to Las Vegas, Nevada, in July 2018. While my wife and kids visited with family one afternoon, I went back to the hotel to rest. Sitting alone by myself, with time to think, I determined that when we returned home, I would speak with Fr. Daniel Gee, the pastor at Saint Rita's, and tell him I wished to be baptized. I assented to the authority of the successor of Saint Peter, Pope Francis, and the authority of the Roman Catholic Church then and there in the three-star hotel room, the scent of stale tobacco invading my nostrils, on a hot summer day by myself and without fanfare of any kind. It simply made sense to me. I then placed an order online that will strike non-Mormon readers as odd but will be immediately recognizable as significant to the initiated. My order on July 28, 2018, read: "Hanes Men's 10-Pack Boxer Briefs with Comfort Flex Waistband; 2 × 5 Pack Fruit of the Loom Men's Stay-Tucked V-Neck T-Shirt". I stopped wearing the temple garments from then onward. There was no looking back.

That same day, major outlets across the world reported that Pope Francis had accepted the resignation from the College of Cardinals of Theodore McCarrick, former archbishop of Washington, D.C., and one of the most powerful and well-known Catholics in the world. The Holy See, it was reported, removed him from public ministry in June 2018 after an internal investigation concluded there were credible allegations that he sexually abused an altar boy during preparations for Christmas Mass at Saint Patrick's Cathedral in New York in the early 1970s.

Reports about the scandal broke in June, but the story began to dominate the news cycle. Non-Catholic friends to whom I reported I was becoming Catholic questioned, "Really? Right now?" It was a fair point. It seemed like the worst possible timing, as some of the Church's filthiest laundry was being publicly aired, including numerous reports that high-ranking Catholic clergy across the globe had been aware of the allegations for decades. It was painful and awkward for me, and I was not even Catholic. I had nothing but empathy for the countless Catholics who were infuriated by what seemed like a repeat of the sex abuse scandal of the early 2000s, complete with coverups and promises this was done and over with, to say nothing of the victims of the horrid abuse—a scandal that got worse and worse with time as more was revealed about McCarrick's case. Still, I was unmoved in my determination to become Catholic. I had read far too much Catholic history by that point, warts, blunders, errors, and all, and knew that while the Church was certainly in the midst of a major crisis in this regard—her moral witness to the world completely undermined by her apparent complicity in unspeakable crimes—she had been through two millennia's worth of difficulty, and this was a cross we had to bear as Catholics at this time. So I pressed forward.

Fr. Gee and I began meeting privately on Saturday mornings for about an hour at a time. After a visit or two, he told me that there was no need for me to undergo the Rite of Christian Initiation for Adults (RCIA)—a formal instructional class for those thinking of becoming Catholic or returning to the faith, which ends with baptism at the Easter Vigil Mass. Rather, he said he could authorize my baptism without the classes based on the knowledge of Catholicism I exhibited. By that point, I had read hundreds and hundreds of pages of the Church Fathers, a number of books about Catholicism, and most of the Catechism (the big one). To make sure I understood some key points well, he would assign readings to me each week from the smaller *Compendium of the Catechism*. I could bring all my questions and concerns to him for us to discuss, and he would briefly give me private instruction in the faith. Father Gee had little experience with Mormonism, and I suspect he anticipated my putting up a fight on things like Mary, the saints, the relationship between faith and works, and other hot points for traditional Protestants. But my readings through the Fathers had moved my mind far beyond the ability to quarrel with antiquity. Beyond some basic review, our time was mostly spent on my biggest concern: How was I supposed to do all this with my wife still raising the kids Mormon? Fr. Gee, with wisdom, prudence, and pastoral insight that I imagine only comes from being neck-deep in people's most intimate and painful problems for decades, helped me chart a patient course.

As my baptismal date neared, I knew there was only one more step to go. To spare my wife pain, stress, and embarrassment, I was determined to avoid at all costs being called into what, at the time, was called a "disciplinary council" of the Mormon Church, which would likely result in my excommunication. Paragraphs 6.7.3 and 6.7.4 of the church's official handbook for leaders at the time read that such a council was "mandatory ... when evidence suggests that a member" has committed "apostasy", which, among other things, was defined as "formally join[ing] another church and advocat[ing] its teachings". I was still attending church with my wife to help with the kids during the main meeting each week and planned to continue doing so after I was baptized Catholic—solely as a means of helping, not as a means of worshiping. But it seemed to me that I was running a risk, as I could not rightly conceal that I was Catholic—nor do I have the personality not to, as the handbook states it, "advocate" the teachings of the Church to which I would soon belong.

I therefore determined that I would resign my membership in the Mormon Church and ask, in Mormon parlance, to have my "records removed". I called the bishop of the ward and asked him to come to our home one evening. I explained to him that I needed him to help me resign and remove my records, and I understood he was the person through whom such requests went. He confirmed that was the case. Unlike horror stories I have heard from others who have attempted to leave the church in this manner, I found no resistance, only understanding and genuine concern from our Mormon bishop. I think he saw there was no wavering in me. He asked me a question that was difficult to answer, because it is a question that actually only makes sense to a believing Mormon and is out of context from a Catholic perspective: "Have you received a testimony from the Holy Ghost that Catholicism is true?" In the strictest sense of his question, the answer was clearly no. But the question is loaded, as it presupposes that this is in fact how God tells people to join a church. I answered that God had indicated to me that this was the right thing to do in a way that makes sense within the framework of Catholicism. He did not try to stop me, but he did ask me to take some time first to consider formally staying a member of the church so that it would not impact Carly's temple blessings. As he explained, any future children would not be sealed to anyone (he was unaware that we had just found out Carly was pregnant—another consequence of my decision to become Catholic). And he offered an explanation of the result of Carly's sealing to our current children that struck me as odd and ad hoc. The effect between my children and *me*, however was clear: our sealings would be removed, and I would no longer have any claim on them as my children in eternity. I told the bishop I would think about it, although as my wife said, just about as soon as he closed the door, it clearly wouldn't be the right thing for me formally to "remain" Mormon while in reality being Catholic.

A week later, September 16, 2018, I arose early and dashed off the following letter and dropped it on the bishop's desk after church:[70]

Dear Bishop ...:

I wanted to thank you for coming to visit with Carly and me last Sunday, September 9, 2018. I appreciate your care and concern for me and my family. You are a good man.

Though I took into sincere consideration your suggestion that I formally remain a member of the Church of Jesus Christ of Latter-day Saints ("the Church"), I cannot in good conscience do such a thing. I think that in an effort to ensure that we had as pleasant a conversation as possible, I may have understated my conviction and intention to be baptized Catholic. So, to be clear, let me explain. I have been intensely "investigating" (to use

---

[70] I wrote the letter over just a few hours, and so I have corrected a few typos as well as broken up some paragraphs for ease of reading here.

a familiar term) the Catholic faith for more than a year. I have been attending Mass without miss for about six months. I have met with priests on several occasions to discuss numerous issues, doctrinal, pastoral, and personal. I am converted, not converting.

Effective as of the date of this letter, I hereby resign my membership in the Church. No thirty-day waiting period is necessary for me to consider this decision. I am fully informed and aware of the alleged consequences the Church attaches to this decision. Nor is there any further need for us to visit about the matter in person. I trust you will speedily handle all administrative matters on the Church's end, which I consider to be only formality at this point. I will be baptized Catholic before the year's end, so I respectfully ask that you take care of the matter promptly.

When you asked me whether I had a spiritual confirmation of the truthfulness of Catholicism, I said yes but was a bit nuanced in my response because while the answer is yes, it is not like the "spiritual confirmation" you are talking about. Please do not take offense, but you have to understand that I view Mormon "testimony" as built almost entirely on emotion. It is subjective. It is fideism. St. Paul taught, "Prove all things; hold fast that which is good." (1 Thess. 5:21). As I commented, Mormonism taught me much "good" to which I do still "hold fast." But I fear that honest examination of its history and tenets do not hold up. Members of the Church are explicitly taught to ignore "unanswered questions" and to be "a bit more patien[t]" Dieter F. Uchtdorf, Come, Join with Us (Oct. 2013 General Conference). But there are clear answers to the questions at issue (which I will briefly discuss further below).

The point is, I am now Catholic and there is no hesitancy in my belief. I have not had any individual emotional experience that was God's answer to my prayers. Rather, I have seen and quietly felt his Divine Providence shaping my life and leading me to truth both in my mind and in my heart, but in a way that is palpably distinct from my former beliefs in Mormonism. I am finally no longer asked to believe in things for which not only is there no evidence, but which the evidence strongly condemns on fair inspection. Nor am I in need of any spiritual insurance policy (i.e., hanging on to formal Church membership)— I am either right or wrong and I will stand before Christ to be judged of my decision when I die. And I would be loath to stand before him "neither cold nor hot," to be "spew[ed] ... out of [his] mouth." (Revelation 3:16).

Let me be clear:

I believe in one God, the Father almighty, Maker of heaven and earth, and of all things, visible and invisible. And in one Lord Jesus Christ, the only begotten Son of God. Born of the Father, before all ages. God of God: Light of Light: true God of true God. Begotten, not made, consubstantial with the Father, by whom all things were made. Who, for us men and for our salvation, came down from heaven and became incarnate by the Holy Ghost of the Virgin Mary and was made man. He was crucified also for us, suffered under Pontius Pilate, and was buried. And the third day, He rose again according to the Scriptures. And ascended into heaven, and sitteth at the right hand of the Father. And He shall come again with glory to judge both the living and the dead, of whose kingdom there shall be no end. And in the Holy Ghost, the Lord and Giver of Life, Who proceeds from the Father and the Son. Who, together with the Father and the Son, is adored and glorified: Who spoke by the prophets. And in one, holy, Catholic and Apostolic Church. I confess one baptism for the remission of sins. And I look for the resurrection of the dead. And the life of the world to come. Amen.

There were three further points I wanted to make clear through this letter in response to your sincere (and much appreciated) conversation with me and Carly last week.

First, you told me that in your opinion, I was not in "apostasy," though I suggested I was or might be because

I affirmatively deny the core doctrines of the Church that form its unique theology. The Church's ecclesial definition of apostasy is up to the Church, and I will trust your assessment. As of the signing of this letter, I am no longer a member of the Church, so the point is moot. But you seemed to attach to that definition a contingency—the idea that I would not "lead others away" or "destroy faith" (I am paraphrasing, but those strike me as close to the words you used). Let me be unmistakable. I have no intention of not fully, actively, and vocally living the true faith established by Christ and kept alive in Sacred Scripture and Sacred Tradition through the authoritative and inerrant teaching of the Magisterium of the one, holy, Catholic and Apostolic Church. I am as free to speak, write, comment, teach, preach, or think the Christian faith as you are with respect to the faith you profess. Whatever consequences attach to that freedom, I fully accept, but I also expect that the Church will recognize that freedom.

Second, you suggested that in your experience, people leave the Church over history or "sin." I was unsure if you were trying to insinuate something by that, and so I offered up the point that other than the fact that I affirmatively deny Mormon doctrine, I have not done anything warranting excommunication. But lest there be any confusion, let me make it abundantly clear: we are all sinners. It is not that we have all committed sin, which we have; it is that we are all *sinners* (present, active, ongoing tense). So in that sense, yes, I will fully admit, I am in sin. But a desire to abandon the Church's moral teachings never has had anything to do with my decision, and to the extent that is the suggestion, that strikes me as contrary to common experience, good will, and the teachings of at least some of the Brethren. *See* Uchtdorf, *supra*.

Third, and finally, you are correct that this has to do with "history," but this is not about "mistakes of imperfect people." *Id*. That is a silly reason to leave a faith, and unfortunately, it is also a straw-man characterization used to often make it seem like people who leave the Church just expected too much of its leaders. *See, e.g.*, Neil L. Andersen, *Faith Is Not by Chance, but by Choice* (Oct. 2015 General Conference) ("[G]ive Brother Joseph a break!").

The reality is, a fair reading of credible historians and primary sources (not pseudo-apologetics authored by Church employees) is straightforward.

I then laid out my case for why the church was not true. I ended admitting, "I am no scriptural scholar; I am not a theologian; I am not a professional historian, nor an expert in patristics. But there are, to my mind, very good reasons for my decision."

Six days later, I received the following letter from Salt Lake City:

Dear Brother Christiansen,

This letter is to notify you that, in accordance with your request, your name has been removed from the membership records of The Church of Jesus Christ of Latter-day Saints.

Should you desire to become a member of the Church in the future, the local bishop or stake president in your area will be happy to help you.

Sincerely,
Confidential Records

That was it. When I reported the news of my decision to my family, they reacted graciously, content at least that I was doing what I believed to be right, even if a bit bewildered at a decision that seemed to come from nowhere and without much explanation. One close friendship wound up deeply marred, and it is still in recovery. Yet, by God's grace, unlike the decisions of many others who have sacrificed much to join the Catholic Church, mine came with minimal fallout.

I became Catholic six weeks later, on the feast of Saint Charles Borromeo, choosing, perhaps predictably, Saint Thomas More as my patron. He is the patron saint of lawyers, politicians, and statesmen, but my choice was deeper than that. He seemed to me a sort of quiet friend who had long been standing in the background of my life. I first came to know of him in my most ardently believing days as a Mormon, and despite his belief in what I could only see as a Church fallen in apostasy. He had a great impact on me. His determination to do what was right, unswervingly, to the point of the loss of his fame, fortune, good reputation, and ultimately, life, stood as a powerful testament of integrity that I committed to emulate throughout my life. Having made the swim from the Susquehanna to the Tiber, I can only hope that through God's grace I can, as Saint Thomas prayed, set the world at naught, and ultimately die, as Saint Thomas died, God's good servant.

EPILOGUE

ON JUNE 12, 2021, I stood with a small group of friends in the baptistery of Saint Rita Catholic Church in Alexandria, Virginia. Our five children had all been baptized Catholic by that point with their mother's blessing, and they all stood just behind me, gawking at the scene: their mother, leaning over the font, water poured over her head, professing before the priest belief in the one, holy, Catholic, and apostolic Church. She was baptized with our newborn, our sixth child, Peter Ambrose. We have come home, 2,070 days from that night when I broke my wife's heart and threw our lives into spiritual chaos and embarked on a journey I did not even realize I was on.

I have deep admiration, respect, and love for countless members of the Church of Jesus Christ of Latter-day Saints. Although I empathize with those who leave the church and become embittered—anger is a natural emotion to feel when you pass through the sense of betrayal that often comes with learning about Mormon history—I could never join in with the crowds who seem bent on denying that anything good comes from Mormonism. Such a view is obviously false. As they say, God writes straight with crooked lines, and his grace brought much good into my life while I was Mormon. The Mormon sense of community, their commitment to one another, is likely unparalleled in modern religious history. Mormons will drop just about anything to help a neighbor in need, including those who are not of their faith. But goodness in these senses, goodness shared in varying degrees by many faiths and many people without faith at all, is not the measure of the claims a church makes. As this book, I hope, illustrates, for myself, I reached a definite point at which I could no longer make any more sense of Mormonism and came away with the definitive conclusion that, whatever else it was, the Church of Jesus Christ of Latter-day Saints was not what it claimed to be. Others continue to find meaning there, although I cannot help but feel it is at the steep expense of all but redefining what Mormonism is. On the other hand, that may be appropriate. It may be the most truly Mormon thing there is—to continue in constant intellectual and spiritual revolution. I could simply no longer come along for that ride. Rather, through what I take to be Providence and others take to be accident, folly, or delusion, I have found Jesus Christ, order, rationality, and deep fulfillment in the Catholic Church.

I hope that in these pages, Catholics and other Christians might come away with a better understanding of the perspective from which Mormons are coming. I would not expect my experience to be a universal one, but in my discussions with many others who have left the church (whether they joined another religion or abandoned religion altogether), I have found that my experience with Mormonism and my own reasons for believing in it as I did are common enough. So, for the non-Mormon audience, without painting in too broad strokes, the sketch of my life can perhaps help you empathize more fully with those coming from the Mormon tradition.

For Mormons who read this, I am sure many can find fault and even tragedy in my story. Some may criticize me as having foolishly overlooked the advice of modern-day prophets, such as Howard Hunter, who warned against equating "strong emotion or free-flowing tears ... with the presence of the Spirit".[1] My response is twofold. First, I think anyone looking objectively at both the teachings and practice of Mormonism would correctly conclude that the church strongly emphasizes that a testimony is a matter of feeling, particularly whenever there is a conflict between what our intellect tells us about the church's truthfulness and what our feelings tell us about the same. Second, in any event, supposing for the moment that I was simply mistaken from Mormonism's own point of view, then my next answer is this: it is fair to say, at least, that I *truly believed* I had a testimony, that I *thought I knew* the church and its claims were true by the power of the Holy Ghost. To paraphrase Saint John Henry Newman: If any Mormon says in consequence that I had been converted in a wrong way, I cannot help that now.[2]

[1] Howard W. Hunter, *Teachings of the Presidents of the Church: Howard W. Hunter* (Salt Lake City: Church of Jesus Christ of Latter-day Saints, 2015), chap. 22, https://abn.churchofjesuschrist.org/study/manual/teachings-of-presidents-of-the-church-howard-w-hunter/chapter-22-teaching-the-gospel?lang=eng.

[2] John Henry Newman, *Apologia Pro Vita Sua* (New York: Penguin Books, 1994), 183.

APPENDIX

Some Recommended Readings in Mormon History

Brodie, Fawn. *No Man Knows My History: The Life of Joseph Smith.* 2nd ed. New York: Vintage Books, 1995.

Bushman, Richard. *Joseph Smith: Rough Stone Rolling,* reprint edition. New York: Vintage Books, 2005.

Compton, Todd. *In Sacred Loneliness: The Plural Wives of Joseph Smith.* Salt Lake City: Vintage Books, 1997.

Marquardt, H. Michael, "Response to Translation and Historicity of the Book of Abraham". Accessed March 18, 2022. https://user.xmission.com/~research /mormonpdf/responseboa.pdf.

Palmer, Grant. *An Insider's View of Mormon Origins.* Salt Lake City: Signature Books, 2002.

Prince, Gregory. *David O. McKay and the Rise of Modern Mormonism.* Salt Lake City: University of Utah Press, 2005.

Prince, Gregory. *Leonard Arrington and the Writing of Mormon History.* Salt Lake City: University of Utah Press, 2016.

Quinn, D. Michael, *Early Mormonism and the Magic World View.* 2nd ed. Salt Lake City: Signature Books, 1998.

Quinn, D. Michael. "LDS Church Authority and New Plural Marriages, 1890–1904". *Dialogue: A Journal of Mormon Thought* 18, no. 1 (Spring 1985): 9–105.

Quinn, D. Michael, *The Mormon Hierarchy: Extensions of Power*. Salt Lake City: Signature Books, 1997.

Quinn, D. Michael, *The Mormon Hierarchy: Origins of Power*. Salt Lake City: Signature Books, 1994.

Ritner, Robert K. *The Joseph Smith Egyptian Papyri: A Complete Edition*. Salt Lake City: Signature Books, 2013.

Ritner, Robert K. " 'Translation and Historicity of the Book of Abraham]—A Response' ". The Oriental Institute. Accessed March 18, 2022. https://oi.uchicago.edu/sites/oi.uchicago.edu/files/uploads/shared/docs/Research_Archives/Translation%20and%20Historicity%20of%20the%20Book%20of%20Abraham%20final-2.pdf

Roberts, B.H. *Studies of the Book of Mormon*. 2nd ed. Edited by Brigham Madsen. Salt Lake City: Signature Books, 1992.

Vogel, Dan. *Early Mormon Documents*. 5 vols. Salt Lake City: Signature Books, 1996.

Vogel, Dan. *Joseph Smith: The Making of a Prophet*. Salt Lake City: Signature Books, 2004.